EBURY PRESS

OPERATION KHUKRI

Major General Rajpal Punia, YSM, an alumnus of Sainik School, Chittorgarh, was selected for the National Defence Academy, Khadakwasla, at the age of sixteen. He was commissioned into the Indian Army on 9 June 1984 and joined 14 Mechanised Infantry (16 Jammu and Kashmir Rifles). General Punia was the orchestrator of Operation Khukri while commanding a company as part of a United Nations Peacekeeping mission in Sierra Leone. He commanded the oldest brigade of the Indian Army along the Line of Actual Control. He attended the National Defence College course in Thailand, and the United Nations Senior Mission Leaders' Course in Japan. He has the honour of commanding the prestigious Armoured Divison. Under his command, he successfully controlled the 'Jat agitation' of 2016 and vacated the Dera of Ram Rahim in Sirsa. He has served over thirty-five years in the Indian Army, and counting. He is a fine orator and has been penning down his military experiences since the very beginning of his career. He has numerous articles and research papers to his name. This is his first book.

Damini Punia is the proud daughter of a brave soldier and wife of a Bengal Sapper Officer. She is an alumna of Army Public School, Dhaula Kuan, Delhi, and Lady Shri Ram College, Delhi University. She is the official commentator of the Republic Day parade of our nation at Rajpath. She finds writing to be very liberating. This is her maiden attempt as an author.

ADVANCE PRAISE FOR *OPERATION KHUKRI*

'*Operation Khukri* is a fascinating and gripping account of one of the finest United Nations Peacekeeping operations, undertaken in Sierra Leone, West Africa, during 2000. It is the story of 233 Indian Army officers and men, who were besieged for over three months without any replenishment or resupplies, encircled by rebels of the Revolutionary United Front (RUF). The RUF demanded the surrender of all UN peacekeepers, including a British and a Russian officer, but the troops of the Indian garrison at Kailahun, displaying "nerves of steel and an indomitable spirit", refused to lay down their arms. As the Additional Director, General Military Operations, I was masterminding "Operation Khukri" and ensuring that Major Punia and his garrison were provided all possible support, including gunship helicopters of our air force and long-range artillery, so as to make this force capable of undertaking a fighting withdrawal rather than surrender. I could not take my eyes off this engrossing narrative. This book is recommended to our soldiers and countrymen, and also to all UN peacekeepers, as it very eloquently describes an operation, one of the most outstanding in the annals of UN Peacekeeping history, where soldiers of the Indian Army chose death over cowardice, dignity over two meals and honour over freedom'—General J.J. Singh (retd), former Governor of Arunachal Pradesh, and former Chief of the Army Staff

'Operation Khukri was conducted by the Indian peacekeeping contingent during my tenure as Army Chief. This is an inspiring story based on the personal experience of an Indian military peacekeeper in the deep jungles of Sierra Leone. It is about his involvement in winning the hearts and minds of the locals, negotiating peace and then leading a fighting break-out when his camp of 233 soldiers was surrounded, for over two months, by armed rebels. When faced with conflict, his soldierly mindset and devotion to duty scored over his moral conscience'—General V.P. Malik, PVSM, AVSM, ADC, former Chief of the Army Staff

'It is a matter of privilege and personal pride for me to write a few words on the military heroes of the country, who rendered their heroic services not only for safeguarding the sovereignty of India but also beyond our borders, in far-flung Kailahun, Sierra Leone, West Africa, in 2000. I express my deep gratitude towards the members of the armed forces and their families, for their courage and sacrifice while serving for the United Nations during Operation Khukri, led by Major Rajpal Punia (now Major General). I congratulate Major General Punia, one of the 233 soldiers who worked tirelessly to shape the brave story of Operation Khukri. This book is a befitting tribute to our immortal soldiers who laid down their lives to keep the tricolour flying high. It will surely be a treasure trove of inspiration for the coming generations, the armed forces and for all those who wish to learn about the heroic deeds of our brave soldiers like Havildar Krishan Kumar, Sena Medal (posthumous). I appreciate the efforts made by Major General Punia in the making of this book and wish him all the success in his future endeavours'—Droupadi Murmu, Governor of Jharkhand

'*Operation Khukri* is an important, distinguished and educative account of the trials and triumphs of a real war hero on the epic battlefields of Sierra Leone'—Phagu Chauhan, Governor of Bihar

'*Operation Khukri* is a gem of a book that deserves to be read by every Indian. It will surely keep the reader hooked till the end. Brilliant narration. *Operation Khukri* signals our glorious victory and enhances our respect for our armed forces'—Jagdeep Dhankhar, Governor of West Bengal

'Fighting the deadliest rebel force is not easy, and doing so on their own turf is difficult 100 times over. But our 233 brave soldiers fought their way to freedom. This book is the epitome of valour and pride of our soldiers in Olive Green'—Randeep Hooda, actor and equestrian

'I was a military observer at Kailahun during the May 2000 crisis and was held hostage by the RUF rebels along with Major Punia. I was witness to the heroic and responsive leadership of Major Punia in handling the crisis. Major Punia's efforts in Kailahun carved a glorious path for India–Nepal relations. It was because of his diligent endeavour that all peacekeepers and military observers returned to their respective countries with honour and dignity'—Major General Suresh Kumar Karki, Suprawal Jana Sewa Shree, Gorkha Dakchhinbahu, Nepal Army

'It is rare for Indian soldiers on a peacekeeping mission to first become prisoners of the local militia and then, after months of captivity—without much food or sleep—to fight their way out of their camp, surrounded by armed rebels in the jungles of Africa. This required a daring plan, tenacity, professionalism and sheer cold courage. Major (now General) Rajpal Punia, and his determined band of officers and men from 14 Mechanised Infantry and a Gorkha Unit (5/8 GR), did precisely that, to create a legacy that will perhaps never be emulated in the foreseeable future. Hats off to Rajpal Punia and his band of very brave men. Major Punia's leadership, despite enormous pressures, in confronting multiple factors in war-torn but diamond-rich Sierra Leone in West Africa, was remarkable. He sought peace to the very end but not a compromise, as surrender for him and his men was not an option. Thus, he eventually led his men in a dramatic break-out from his camp, surrounded by heavily armed rebels, to a rendezvous with his headquarters. Before doing so, Major Punia exercised astute political–diplomatic skills (normally not the forte of a soldier) while keeping as his primary aim the preservation of India's dignity and the honour of the tricolour. It is a story that every Indian—especially army officers—must read and learn from. This is a tale of leadership and valour, superbly narrated by Damini Punia. It is the stuff that legends are made of'—Maroof Raza, defence analyst, and consulting editor, Times Network

OPERATION KHUKRI

THE TRUE STORY BEHIND THE INDIAN ARMY'S MOST SUCCESSFUL MISSION AS PART *of* THE UNITED NATIONS

MAJOR GENERAL RAJPAL PUNIA
DAMINI PUNIA

EBURY
PRESS

An imprint of Penguin Random House

EBURY PRESS

USA | Canada | UK | Ireland | Australia
New Zealand | India | South Africa | China

Ebury Press is part of the Penguin Random House group of companies
whose addresses can be found at global.penguinrandomhouse.com

Published by Penguin Random House India Pvt. Ltd
4th Floor, Capital Tower 1, MG Road,
Gurugram 122 002, Haryana, India

Penguin
Random House
India

First published in Ebury Press by Penguin Random House India 2021

Copyright © Major General Rajpal Punia and Damini Punia 2021

ISBN 9780143453369

Typeset in Adobe Garamond Pro by Manipal Technologies Limited, Manipal
Printed at Thomson Press India Ltd, New Delhi

To my grandfather,
Shri Chimna Ram Ji Punia.
I am who I am because of you.

To the army behind the soldier, my wife, Anita. My deepest
gratitude to her, without whom this book wouldn't have been
written. Thank you for being the first person who believed in me
as a writer. Thank you for teaching me how to follow my heart.
She has been my pillar of strength, my core and, above all, my
biggest cheerleader since 1989.

—Major General Rajpal Punia

Contents

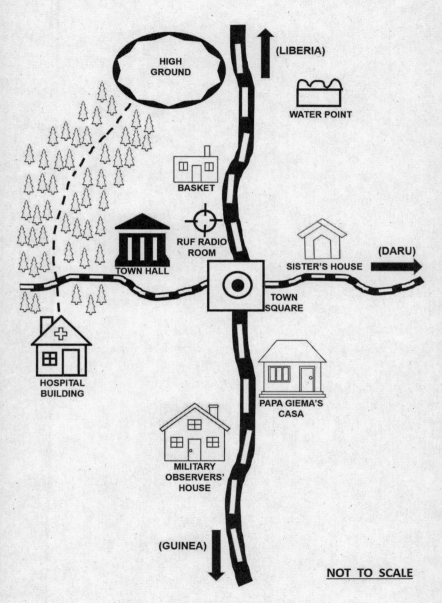

Layout of Kailahun

Foreword

Sierra Leone, a small ex-British colony in West Africa, is a picturesque nation with abundant natural resources but lack of freedom among the people to revel in the treasure that nature had to offer. Sierra Leone had been battered by years of civil war, military coups and been a victim of a rebel movement, whose motives were dubious and methods plainly vicious. Under the grip of endless horror and tragedy, around 50,000 people died in Sierra Leone, with more than a million displaced, and peace eluded the nation for over nine years.

Way back in 2000, as a novice reporter, I had the opportunity to visit Sierra Leone and interact with the Indian peacekeepers in Daru. Through my presence in the war-torn nation, I could be a via media between India and the Indians in Sierra Leone. Being in Daru, I learnt about the 233 Indian peacekeepers who were cordoned off in Kailahun, the heartland of the Revolutionary United Front (RUF).

These 233 soldiers, under the command of Major Rajpal Punia, braved over two months of confinement at the hands of the RUF, without basic necessities available to them. Stationed in Daru, I heard the tales of the 'Tiger', aka Major Rajpal Punia, who had refused to lay down weapons before the rebel forces even at the risk of his life.

Day in and day out, I could see peacekeepers of all other nations, without arms and stripped off their uniforms, being transported to Liberia in ramshackle trucks. But the Indians did not surrender, the Indians were brave.

As luck would have it, I had the privilege of a rendezvous with Major (now Major General) Rajpal Punia. It was a transcontinental meeting in Daru, after his successful completion of Operation Khukri, which he had orchestrated to a T. Operation Khukri was the epitome of the grit, determination and valour of our Indian Army soldiers. The 233 soldiers of 14 Mechanised Infantry and 5/8 Gorkha Rifles fought against the curveball that the RUF threw at them. And when peace was no longer an option, the Indian soldiers fought, and how—for the dignity of their uniforms and the honour of our nation.

This book is the reality of a soldier I happen to admire a lot. I am honoured to have been a part of one of the most successful operations of the Indian Army on foreign Soil. Years later, in 2018, I met Major General Rajpal Punia, Yudh Seva Medal, at the Republic Day press conference, which was chaired by him. During the press conference, I felt as though time had stood still, as though it was just yesterday that I was interviewing this brave young officer in the Blue Beret who had returned from the clutches of the deadliest rebel force in the world—to be present that day, heading the press conference, with me sitting at the other end of the podium.

I take great pleasure in writing this foreword for Major General Rajpal Punia. It's unfortunate how we Indians were not aware of this brave act of the Indian Army on alien soil as part of the United Nations. This book will surely inspire the youth of our country and tell the world the saga of a soldier who was responsible for 233 beating hearts and had to ensure that zero caskets returned home. This spine-chilling narrative will surely keep you gripped till the last word.

Sir, it was an honour to have been a part of this journey of yours.

Jai Hind!

Gaurav C. Sawant
Senior Executive Editor, India Today

Introduction

On 24 March 2020, I caught the flight to Patna at the eleventh hour. Delhi was slowly getting submerged under the dreadful coronavirus pandemic, and the Prime Minister had ordered a complete lockdown in India. My father was posted at Danapur Cantonment, fifteen kilometres from Patna, a place unheard of. I didn't know what to expect, but the fact that our abode was on the banks of the holy river Ganges was enough to get me all excited about this trip. Being optimistic about returning in a week's time, I packed my stuff and rushed to the market to get a travel cage for my companion Noddy, a three-month-old beagle. And so, we embarked on this adventure with masks around our faces, gleaming eyes peeping through, a small strolley for me and a mini rucksack for Noddy.

We reached Danapur hours after the sun shifted west and hence couldn't discern much in terms of the area around. The following morning was surreal beyond words as we sat on the gazebo overlooking the Ganga, feeling the cool breeze in our hair. From that moment on, the gazebo became our spot. Noddy would enjoy calling out to the boats that sailed across. A week switched to a month and a month turned into two—Noddy and I were still in Danapur. As the days of summer decreased our gazebo time to half, I decided to dive deep into our storerooms, filled with endless memories and souvenirs from our travels across the country. Every army home is filled with an abundance of black iron boxes covered in the dust of nostalgia stacked one over the other. The snowy numbers painted on them keep multiplying as we move from one station to another with piles of stories, mementos and memories.

While riffling through the treasure trove, I got my hands on a diary bound in brown leather, cracked and dry with age. The year '2001' was engraved on its top right corner. It smelt faintly of naphthalene balls (something that is found in the box of every army soldier). The pages were crumbly, and what remained of the diary's original stitching was barely holding it together. A faint scrawl on the inside of the leather cover declared that it belonged to Major Rajpal Punia (my father). The story of Kailahun ran through these pages in bleached ink. The captivating minutiae of Operation Khukri had me completely engrossed. The diary was like a motion picture flashing before my eyes, with moments of pride, laughter, sorrow and, most of all, respect—respect for the Olive Green and the Indian Army.

Major Rajpal Punia led Operation Khukri, one of the most successful operations of the Indian Army as part of the United Nations Peacekeeping in Sierra Leone, West Africa, in the year 2000. It's a spine-tingling story, of 233 Indian Army soldiers who were cordoned off for three months without food. They had not spoken to anyone back home. There was no news about their families, and yet the *josh* (zeal) was high. The air of uncertainty hovered over the cloistered soldiers, but their pride for their motherland was intact.

We Indians today owe our high station, in relation to other nations, to these brave hearts, most of whom go unnoticed in a country with over a hundred crore people. The world had to know of the Kailahun story, and that is how the idea of this book took shape.

The book is indeed a restructuring of Major Punia's memories and an attempt to highlight the courage and valour of every soldier donning the olive-green uniform in India. This book portrays the magic of the camouflage uniform, where the swirly patterns of patriotism are stitched together with the thread of the soldier's courage and immense love for their home country. This book is certainly special to me as a daughter, but it should be so for every citizen of India, as this was one of the most successful missions of the Indian Army in the blue beret of the United Nations. It is truly unfortunate that people are not aware of an operation that transpired a year after the Kargil War, an operation where soldiers chose death over cowardice, dignity over two meals and honour over freedom. The Indian soldiers fought both mentally and physically on alien soil, against an unknown enemy, a war not for territory or peaks but a war so that the tricolour could flutter with pride over millions of peaks in India.

This book is dedicated to Havildar* Krishan Kumar, Sena Medal (posthumous), the only gallant warrior we lost in the operation. The debt that we owe to Havildar Krishan Kumar's family can never be repaid. India owes its existence to Havildar

---

* A non-commissioned officer in the Indian Army corresponding to a sergeant.

Krishan Kumar and many other fallen comrades who didn't let the honour of the tricolour dwindle.

To all the soldiers who sacrificed their lives for the honour of our nation. To every tricolour casket that landed in every city, town and village in India. To the families who lost their loved ones so ours could be close to us. India is truly the Nation of the Brave.

Jai Hind

Damini Punia

Preface

It is a heartfelt confession that the intent behind this book is to share with the world the tales of tenacity and valour along with the horrendous experience of encounter with death endured by 233 Indian peacekeepers, day in and day out, for three long months in Kailahun.

The Kailahun story is very close to my heart, and for this reason I shall let my emotions take control of the steering wheel, guiding the events as they unfolded. I would fail in my duty as a Company Commander towards every soldier at Kailahun if I don't give shape to the chronology of the developments that manifested during the 'May 2000' crisis. The Revolutionary United Front (RUF) had held thousands of United Nations peacekeepers hostage, but the Indian peacekeepers at Kailahun stood their ground, displaying nerves of steel and an indomitable spirit, ready to face death rather than lay down weapons before the rebels. For us, our honour was paramount.

During that mission, my belief in destiny was reinforced manifold, and even today, when I look back, I express my gratitude towards God for paving the way for me to reach Kailahun. I thank every soldier who was in that crisis with me for being my inspiration. Words fail me, but I'd like to thank Colonel Martin, the Brigade Commander of the rebel RUF brigade located at Kailahun, and the Papa Giema of Kailahun, without whose faith in me I could not have fulfilled my duty towards my brethren soldiers. While doing what I did, I had to pay the enormous price of carrying this emotional baggage to date, and I can probably never wash off the red stains of collateral damage—innocent civilians who lost their lives—as we fought to save the lives of my soldiers, my responsibility.

It is a long, emotional and rather spine-chilling story that I am going to share with you all, leaving the responsibility of judgement on my readers. I assure you that I shall humbly accept your verdict.

Major General Rajpal Punia

#1

Man Proposes, God Disposes

September 1999

I had just moved to Babina, a one-horse town on the banks of
the Betwa River in the Jhansi district of Uttar Pradesh. Prior
to this, I was posted at Tangdhar in Jammu and Kashmir,
a high-altitude terrain along the Line of Control (LoC)
which was very active in low-intensity conflicts. I was the
Brigade Major controlling all the operations, including heavy
firing across the LoC, which used to be rather frequent and
intense. Our brigade was like a jetty into Pakistan, and we
were referred to as the 'Chutney* Brigade', since the Pakistani
bunkers felt they could make chutney out of us as per
their whims.

    We were stationed across the Shamshabari mountain ridge,
which generally was the baseline for the LoC. Our location
was so precarious that the Pakistanis dominated all the peaks

---

* Smashed.

overlooking our brigade. Incidentally, ours was the only brigade that was across the Shamshabari ridge, and it was as if we were always in the soup. I was posted here when the Kargil War was in full swing, and a counter-reaction of the Kargil operation was anticipated in our area. I recollect pushing six battalions, as reinforcement, into the area, which was earlier held by three battalions. I also vividly remember the Adjutant of the Richamar* Battalion pleading with me not to dispatch any more troops since there was no place to even stand in the bunkers.

Broadly speaking, it was three years of high altitude, combating militants, controlling the trans Line of Control firing, which made even a minute's sleep a silken dream, and finally, the last straw being the Kargil operations. All this made the last three years an eventful ride that eventually transformed my vision of the world around me, and those memories were forever etched in my journey of life.

There aren't rainbows without rain, and so these three years did take a heavy toll on my family life. On one side was my call of duty, the fulfilment of an oath to obey all commands, even to the peril of my life, as nation comes first, always and every time. On the other side was the separation from my family which came with its share of agony and heartbreaks. So, after endless days and nights of feeling a little blue, we as a family were really looking forward to finally living together at Babina, where my battalion, 14 Mechanised Infantry (16 Jammu and Kashmir Rifles), was located.

I have always been a staunch believer in the proverb 'Man proposes, God disposes'. People may come up with any

---

* Richamar was the name of the area where the battalion was located and hence the name.

number of ingenious plans, but ultimately, the forces outside our control determine our future course. God's intent started unfolding on my first day at work in Babina when a signal came from the Army Headquarters stating that I was selected for deputation in a United Nations Peacekeeping mission in Sierra Leone, West Africa. Under normal circumstances, it would have been a time to rejoice and celebrate, as all military personnel look forward to such an opportunity because of the accompanying extensive international exposure and, not to forget, a chance to draw a salary in dollars. Yet my heart sank reading the signal, since I could only think of my family's reaction to this news. Truth be told, the previous evening itself I had heard my four-year-old daughter telling her mother, 'Hope Papa will not leave us now.' I had a lump in my throat imagining my daughter's tiny inquisitive eyes questioning as to whether we would be staying together, whether Papa would attend their birthdays and school functions—every blink of her eye was hoping for an affirmative.

My colleagues, oblivious to these facts, insisted on a glass of beer in the officers' mess before heading home, and I somehow agreed, thinking what chilled beer could do to your confidence! At the officers' mess, I told my brother officers that though the drinks were on me, I had decided not to go for the mission. The moment I would decline, one of them would be nominated for the mission, since our Mechanised Infantry Company* had to be commanded by an officer of our own battalion. It was a proud moment for the battalion and, therefore, a piece of news to celebrate.

---

* A company is a subset of a battalion, with three platoons under every company. Each platoon comprises forty soldiers.

On my way home, I contemplated whether to break the news to my family. Eventually, I didn't divulge the information, for the only reason that I didn't have the heart to talk about it; however, to my utter surprise, by then my wife had already learnt about the news. I explained to my wife that I had decided to decline the deputation, and there was no room for second thoughts over this decision. Hearing this, my wife, who has always been our guiding light, reminded me of my singular principle in life, to move with destiny. Being a daughter and a wife of an army officer, she did not want to see her husband shy away from organizational orders. She asked me to follow my 'Uniform Dharam'* of moving wherever the organization posted me, and serve with utmost devotion and sincerity, as always.

I didn't have any logic or words to counter her argument; and honestly, I didn't even want to, since she was beaming with pride, and that was enough to push me for this mission. I remembered the oath which every soldier takes on wearing the uniform, that no matter what the circumstance, he will serve his motherland till his last breath. I embraced her, as though asking for reassurance that our souls would be connected for a lifetime and that absence would only make our hearts grow fonder of each other. Incidentally, that was our first evening in the new house allotted to us at Babina, and I was to leave the following day.

I had to report to Delhi to my newly assigned battalion for the mission, the 5/8 Gorkha Rifles, and jointly we were to establish a new mission in the war-torn country of Sierra Leone in West Africa. A cursory glance at the status of various countries around the globe immediately made it clear that Sierra Leone was

---

* Duty towards the uniform.

one of the poorest countries in the world, further exasperated by years of civil war and military coups. The nation had also long been the victim of a rebel movement called the Revolutionary United Front (RUF), whose intentions were dubious and approach barbaric. Sierra Leone appeared to be in the clutches of endless mayhem, with over 50,000 deaths, millions of people dislodged, gruesome crimes inflicted on women, children and others, including ravishment, arson, mutilation and mass murder. Tranquillity had circumvented Sierra Leone for nine years. Cities and towns were drowning in insecurity, with the supposedly vanquished rebel army indulging in malevolent retributive campaigns against the vulnerable civilian population. After years of turmoil, the Lomé Peace Agreement was like the light at the end of the tunnel for the people of Sierra Leone. The agreement, signed by the RUF in July 1999, stated that the RUF was willing to lay down weapons to a neutral force of the United Nations. Hence, the Indian Army was given the proud privilege to set up a mission in Sierra Leone to aid in establishing peace on alien soil.

A tremendous amount of background preparation takes place at the preliminary stage prior to any mission of this scale and magnitude. For an international mission of the United Nations, orientation and in-depth knowledge of the ethos of the organization were to be imbibed. Hence, the initial two months in Delhi were meant for integration and preparation, and each one of us was cautioned concerning the impending task. That was when the severe routine of physical fitness, training, and also the gathering of all possible information about Sierra Leone, commenced.

Colonel Satish was our Commanding Officer, a thorough gentleman but a man of few words with an impassive facial expression that was enough to put anyone under stress; and his Second-in-Command, Lieutenant Colonel Amit Sharma, was diametrically opposite, yet even he could impose pressure by the sheer variety of expressions, which were a gift from God. The Gorkha Regiment of the Indian Army is allegedly very OG,* while being from the Mechanised Infantry with an entirely disparate environment, we found it an arduous task to blend in, and had to undergo a lot of churning as part of our integration in Delhi. We had to coalesce with the Gorkha Regiment for the mission; hence orders from two different Commanding Officers, located in Delhi and Babina, were to be accommodated.

The Indian Army is an invincible organization, and the soldiers are trained to adapt to the whole nine yards in no time. Luckily for me, my senior-most Subedar† in the company, Fateh Singh, was a gift to mankind, for he exuded positivity and didn't have the unfavourable two-letter word 'No' in his dictionary. Even the young officers in my company, Captain Sudesh, Captain Prashant and Captain Sunil, were self-driven, gallant officers, and the company, being a homogeneous entity comprising soldiers solely from 14 Mechanised Infantry, didn't face any turbulence despite having to camp in tents in Delhi, right behind the Sadar Bazar area of Delhi Cantonment.

As part of our preparations, we were supposed to gather as much information about Sierra Leone as possible, since knowing the ropes would aid our deployment in a far-off land. The entire process of assimilating information was an eye-opener for all of

---

* Olive Green: a term in the Indian Army used for those who excessively abide by rules and protocols.
† Rank in the Indian Army for a Junior Commissioned Officer.

us as the more we learnt about Sierra Leone, the more blessed we felt to have been born in India.

In spite of being the erstwhile wealthiest country in the world, with an abundance of the best-grade diamonds, Sierra Leone lacked basic amenities like electricity and tap water, even in the national capital, Freetown. Nearly 30 per cent of its population were amputees because of the civil war that had gripped the country for over a decade. Countless monstrosities were inflicted on the people by the RUF.

The one similarity between Sierra Leone and India was that, like India, Sierra Leone had been a British colony. It was under British subjugation till as late as April 1961, and when the British left, the local currency, the leone, was equal to the US dollar. But when we went there in 1999, one dollar was equal to 3000 leones.

Geographically speaking, Sierra Leone is a small nation situated in West Africa with a seacoast on the Atlantic Ocean, Guinea to its north and Liberia to the south. Its capital, Freetown, derived its name from the fact that the prosperous countries left the slaves free in this town during the eighteenth century. It's ironic that in the foregone times, the people inhabiting the place were known for being free and out of the clutches of slavery. They were now slaves to their inherent trepidation as, except Freetown, the entire nation was ablaze.

After 1961, post-independence, consecutive governments could not arrest corruption in the country, and by the mid-1980s, corruption was at its peak. That was when Foday Saybana Sankoh, a Corporal in the Sierra Leone Army, started the Revolutionary United Front, with an intent to provide his people a corruption-free nation. Due to this noble ambition, his revolutionary ideas were welcomed by the people of Sierra Leone, and Foday Sankoh was respected for his virtuous initiative. Little did they know that the new outfit they thought would aid in bringing sunshine to their country clouded with the showers of corruption would later turn out to be the cause of the bloodiest war in the history of Sierra Leone.

There is no denying the fact that in its embryonic stage, the RUF did the right amount of work for the betterment of people. Hence, it became quite robust in a brief period. But as they say, power tends to corrupt, and absolute power corrupts absolutely. The RUF was a live example of this. The democratically elected Government of Sierra Leone was overthrown by Foday Sankoh with assistance provided by Charles Taylor, the President of Liberia, a country neighbouring Sierra Leone.

With its burden of unaccountable corruption, Sierra Leone stepped into a civil war, with too many stakeholders along with anarchy and chaos grasping the entire functioning of the country and completely devastating a former peace-loving nation. During that time, the West African countries, under the leadership of Nigeria, formed a conglomerate called ECOMOG (the Economic Community of West African States Monitoring Group) to restore normality in Sierra Leone. Even that failed to control the RUF, and the ECOMOG was brutally defeated by Foday Sankoh and his outfit in the late '90s.

Since then, the RUF had been controlling the entire country, including the diamond areas, and the Government of Sierra Leone, under the presidency of Dr Ahmad Tejan Kabbah, controlled only Freetown. Diamond smuggling by the RUF became the order of the day. As barter, the best weapons and drugs started coming into the RUF's hands, as even the most prosperous countries of the world were involved in this infamous act of diamond smuggling. The situation further deteriorated to the extent that the world had to take note of this. As a result, with the United Nations' intervention, all stakeholders, including the RUF, had to sign the Lomé Peace Agreement in July 1999. As per the agreement rules, the RUF agreed to lay down weapons to a neutral force of the UN, and thereafter a free and fair election was to be conducted in Sierra Leone. As part of this agreement, we were awaiting our induction. Our priority was to get deployed and, thereafter, commence the Disarmament, Demobilization and Rehabilitation Programme (DDR) of the RUF rebels. The DDR process was primarily to reintegrate the rebels into the society by way of training them in different vocations which they could pursue post disarmament. The DDR approach would consequently set the stage for free and fair elections in the country.

As we gathered a considerable amount of information about Sierra Leone, which was an ongoing exercise, our time in Delhi was also spent in the medical examination of every soldier who was part of our contingent. Prior to deployment in any foreign assignment, every soldier must go through a strict medical check-up. The strictness was further reinforced as a result of the medical advisory issued by the United Nations due to life-threatening diseases prevalent in Sierra Leone. Every possible medical test that was feasible in our country back in 1999 was conducted on us. Soldiers who were medically unfit were returned to their units, from where their replacements were dispatched. Time was at a premium, so we requested their respective units to earmark a pool of reserve soldiers and locate them in advance in Delhi, so that movement time could be saved. Medical tests took place on a daily basis, where some samples were given and some reports were received.

There were two categories of soldiers in our camp for ease of selection. The first group was the one detailed for the mission, and the other had soldiers who were part of the 'Reserved for the Mission' group. The soldiers looked forward to this new assignment for various reasons, some for the thrill of travelling by air to a far-off land, while for others, this mission was a chance to improve their financial situation as they would draw handsome salaries.

Usually, evenings were the most dreaded, as all soldiers would anxiously await the arrival of the Company Havildar Major.* He would walk into the camp with the medical reports he had received so far. I cannot begin to explain the divergent nervous energies that surrounded the evening roll call awaiting the announcement of the Company Havildar Major. This scenario in the camp became customary, where some hearts were broken and some new faces with added vigour joined the wagon. I witnessed some of my boys holding their reports and going towards the temple, while on the other side, there were those who packed their bags and asked for railway warrants for the rearward journey.

For me, it was painful to witness this process day in and day out. To top it off, the toughest challenge for me was to pick a new boy from the 'Reserved Category' for every medically unfit boy. To ease the activity and eliminate any scope for bias, I decided to resort to the drawing of lots for 'Reserve Nomination' in our company. Eventually, by the grace of God, the medical selection concluded, and we had the final list of men appointed for the mission. It further enhanced the seriousness and gravity of the training, and other preparations for the mission were accelerated.

---

* Sergeant Major.

By now, two months of the integration phase in Delhi were over, and we had stepped into the twelfth month of 1999, in which the deployment had to commence. During the previous two months, while I was busy preparing for the mission, my wife and kids were adjusting in a new place, and it troubled me immensely that I could not be there to help them settle in. But as they say, not all are high days and holidays. So, we had to stand our ground and let the high waves of separation pass. I realized that post-deployment, I would be away for one year. So, I spoke with my wife and asked her to come to Delhi for a few days. Despite the children's examinations, the tickets were booked, and here I was going to receive them at the New Delhi railway station, truly ecstatic to meet them after a long time. That moment of embracing my wife and kids was the highlight of the Delhi tenure for me. The children were thrilled to ride in a white Gypsy, with 'United Nations' written on it in black, and equally excited to see their Papa in a blue beret. I had arranged for their stay in Taurus Hostel adjacent to our camp in Delhi Cantonment.

Despite my family being in town, I continued with my routine as Load Master. My task as the Load Master encompassed the complete movement of troops and stores from India to Sierra Leone, and this being a new mission, the need of stores was enormous. When Colonel Satish, our Commanding Officer, learnt of my family being in town, he immediately called for me in his office, and that was when the fear of the unknown suddenly gripped me. I wondered what the reason behind this unforeseen invitation was.

I walked into the Commanding Officer's office with oodles of courage and optimism. After a brief pause, the Commanding Officer inquired whether I had taken my family out somewhere in Delhi, to which I immediately replied, 'No, sir.' His face broke into a million-dollar smile when he said that the next day I wouldn't be going for loading at the airport. He ordered me to take my family out sightseeing in Delhi and asked me to take a day off. He also informed me that we would be flying out in a few days from now and that I needed to make the best of the next day as family time.

I returned to Taurus Hostel in high spirits and announced that I had time off for the next twenty-four hours, every minute of which I would spend with my family. It was all smiles that evening. At night, there was a lot of hustle-bustle in the guest room where we were staying, as the children were busy chalking out the next day's programme. The places on their bucket list were India Gate, Appu Ghar, Qutub Minar, and the most exciting place to visit was McDonald's since, in those days, McDonald's existed only in select cities of the country.

Usually, my wife had to wake them up, but wonders never cease—that day, I was surprised to see the kids up early in the morning, with tremendous energy and eagerness for the day ahead. The day was off to a great start with the drive on Rajpath, a visit to Rashtrapati Bhavan, and then to India Gate. Lucky for us that it was December; the weather was conducive for our excursion.

The Delhi of those days was far more beautiful than the city of today, with more trees than buildings, more fresh air than harmful emissions, more people than vehicles, and people with great patience and values. It was indeed a gratifying day, but the highlight for my children was receiving gifts with their Happy Meals at McDonald's. Finally, when we returned to Taurus Hostel that evening, the other occupants at the hostel could sense the joyful tremors resonating through the spring in my children's step and the luminous smile on my wife's face.

Post a rather relaxing day spent with my family after so long, I was back to the grind, controlling the morning loading process at the airstrip at Palam Airport, New Delhi. Coordination between two independent battalions was a laborious task, but fortunately for me, Major Nair, who was a Company Commander in 5/8 Gorkha Rifles, was a great friend of mine, and he went on to become the nucleus of this heterogeneous group for me. Way back in the training days, he was called 'General' Nair in the National Defence Academy, as those Gentleman Cadets who were relegated twice were termed Generals as a status symbol by other cadets in the academy. So, while Nair was six months senior to me, he later passed out as my junior. Major Nair had the responsibility of ensuring that the complete entitled equipment was issued to the Battalion Group, including kits supplied by various contractors who had been supplying to several battalions, inducting in the United Nations, for ages.

Here I must share with you that none of the dresses and kits would fit my tall frame of 6'4". Finally, Major Nair had to get the supplier of individual kits to see me. I remember meeting this young lad, Preet Bawa, who assured me that he would personally cater to my size. Thereafter, Preet would get special boots and dresses, and I was at last glad to have a kit fit my size. Preet would often tell me, 'Sir, you must keep our flag flying high and need not worry about your fittings and kits, as that is my responsibility.' I developed a great bond with this young fellow, thanks to his motivational spirit. Even today, I remember Preet for his memorable statement, 'Sir, keep our national flag flying high.'

Soldiers are supposed to wear their pride, the national flag, on their chests when they go abroad on a United Nations mission. Those pieces of the tricolour pinned to our olive-green uniforms filled our hearts with devotion for our motherland; it was like a patriotic fervour, with every beat of 'Jana Gana Mana', the Indian national anthem, flowing through our veins and our heads held high, representing our honour, India.

The greatest strength of the Indian Army is 'regimentation', a sense of pride and ownership wherein generation after generation it becomes a matter of honour to join the same regiment or battalion as one's father and forefathers. Also, the regiments are like an extended family, where even the elders of a battalion remain connected post relinquishing their command. As part of this connect, Colonel Daya Nand Dahiya (retd), along with Mrs Dahiya, visited us in Delhi to address and motivate the personnel of 14 Mechanised Infantry, who were proceeding for a challenging task as part of United Nations Peacekeeping. Colonel Dahiya was the Commanding Officer of our battalion when I was commissioned, way back in 1984. The first Commanding Officer has a significant impact on the development of every officer. As part of his visit, a quick Sainik Sammelan* was organized. Colonel Dahiya reminded all ranks about the great history of our battalion and asked everyone to do their best in adding the jewel to the crown of the battalion.

An informal tea was organized post the Sainik Sammelan, after which we joined Mrs Dahiya for lunch in the makeshift officers' mess, where, in a one-to-one interaction, Colonel Dahiya inquired about the performance of Captain Prashant, son of Colonel Dahiya, a second-generation officer who was

---

* A practice of addressing the soldiers collectively.

in my company. I reassured him regarding Captain Prashant's performance, telling him that he was a highly motivated officer and physically very tough, who had been drinking five litres of milk daily for quite some time now!

My words—that I would channelize Captain Prashant's energy in the right direction and that he would be back with flying colours—comforted the Colonel. Before leaving, Colonel Dahiya also discussed some matrimonial proposal for Captain Prashant with me, to which I smiled and said, 'Sir, don't be in a hurry to finalize since we are leaving in the next two days. You'll have an entire year to look for the right match.'

The Delhi chapter was finally culminating, and our real journey was about to commence. Delhi was a mix of emotions. On the one hand I was to bid adieu to my family, while on the other we had to move forward with utmost coordination and harmony on a United Nations Peacekeeping mission overseas. It's ironic how the mind of a peacekeeper could race like a tornado on the mere thought of leaving their loved ones behind.

A barakhana* was organized for the contingent on the closing night in Delhi. The camp was surrounded with the bright faces of the soldiers whose spirits were flying high. The boys were to travel to a nation they hadn't heard of before, almost an undiscovered territory. The breeze of excitement gripped the night as everyone retreated to their tents.

---

* A social gathering of company personnel.

#2

Beef Fiasco Mid-Air

28 December 1999

Finally, the momentous day of our departure arrived, and Subedar Fateh got the entire company together. I addressed my boys to wish them a pleasant journey and highlighted the importance of a smooth induction, as, in my opinion, a good outset is half the voyage. I also took a pledge from every soldier to set standards of utmost sincerity and conduct since hereafter, all of us were the ambassadors of our nation. It would be our moral obligation to ensure that no harm was inflicted on India's prestige and that the image of the Indian Army was not tarnished in any way.

Subedar Fateh, apart from being a soldier of the same company, was also a guardian in disguise for his fellow brethren. On his own initiative, he had ensured that every soldier was self-sufficient for at least twenty-four hours, preparing shakar paras[*] and puri sabzi[†] for everyone. This is a standard procedure for

---

[*] Indian sweets.
[†] Deep-fried bread and vegetables.

16

any movement, regardless of the distance to be travelled. The moment I finished talking to the boys, Havildar Krishan Kumar walked up to me. He was emotionally charged up, his nerves swelling with immense love for his country, and his emotions muddling his words spoken in chaste Dogri.[*] Teary-eyed, he expressed his fright at the thought that he might not be able to come back. He touched the soil of our motherland with his hands to symbolically bid farewell to his nation that had made him the soldier he was. He had been my driver for a long time in the battalion, and I knew him intimately as an individual with a very high emotional quotient. I hugged him and dismissed his thoughts as an unnecessary apprehension, and asked him to focus his energy on the mission with paramount optimism.

The convoy of vehicles was lined up for movement from our camp to the international airport, which at that point in time did not have the facilities of the newly constructed Terminal 3 of Indira Gandhi International Airport, New Delhi. The last few minutes at the camp were rather emotional for all of us, with the vibrations of our war cry, 'Bharat Mata Ki Jai (Long Live Mother India)', filling the wind hovering over us with ebullience and glory. The customary prayer was conducted by Sepoy Vinod, who was doing the dual duty of soldier and priest, post which the convoy started rolling with a sea of blue berets. I bifurcated from the convoy to pick up my family, who were also due to leave the same day by train after seeing me off at the airport. My wife did the aarti[†] before we left Taurus Hostel.

----

[*] An Indo–Aryan language spoken in different parts of north-western India.
[†] Hindu religious ritual during which vermilion is applied to the forehead.

I was elated to see the civilian staff of Taurus Hostel, who had lined up to see us off. They had become like an extended family, considering the duration of our stay. Mr Rautela, who was in charge of the civilian staff, wished me luck and took a promise from me to stay with them again on my return. On our way to the airport, I could see the eyes of my better half well up. She held back her tears, and her silent serenity was loud enough to shake my soul to its core. I felt shivers down my spine as I bid goodbye to the love of my life. Her downcast eyes were speaking a thousand words only to convey sincere regret over her decision. However, I knew that she was a very strong lady, and the three-year-long separation had made her even stronger. At that moment, I was short of words. So I took a deep breath and held her hand tightly for the rest of the journey to the airport.

My children were also quiet, as though away with the fairies, probably remembering the struggle their mother had to face head-on over the last three years. Reaching the airport, I could see the excitement of the people present there; they stood stargazing at all the uniformed soldiers in blue berets, with the national colours on our chests. Finally, the time had come to bid farewell to my wife and kids. A silent stare, and just when I remembered my son telling me 'Papa, you are my hero', I couldn't hold my composure any more. I hugged my son and daughter with wet eyes, and my wife joined us in the huddle. I could feel my wife's hand wiping the tears off my eyes—the watery eyes of a soldier in uniform. Indeed, she was the daughter and wife of a soldier.

With fireworks in my chest, I picked up my luggage and moved towards the departure gate. Realizing that I was slightly behind schedule, I looked for Captain Sunil, who was to wait for me at the security check while the rest of the company went through immigration. Captain Sunil quickly guided me through immigration and also informed me that the chartered flight of Air Uzbekistan, which was to take us to Sierra Leone, had already landed. The boarding was quite smooth, and upon realizing the requirement of translating the flight attendant's announcement into Hindi, I deputed Captain Sunil to do the needful. Post the announcement, Captain Sunil was mocked by Captain Prashant for being nominated as the stewardess. No flight in the world would have been in such high spirits as was that Air Uzbekistan flight at that moment in time, with chants of 'Bharat Mata Ki Jai' echoing through the aisle while the aircraft was taxing towards the runway.

The moment I reclined my seat, the thought of not seeing my wife and kids for the next year gave me a sinking feeling. I closed my eyes, covered my face with a handkerchief and felt extremely sad for my children, who had suddenly matured in the last three years. And now, the thought of spending another year away made me feel the guilt of not being able to share their childhood and not being around when they needed me the most. My son took up the responsibilities of the man of the house and promised me that he would look after his mother and sister the way I used to. I was worried only about one thing: that my duty towards my country should in no way snatch my children's carefree childhood. When other dads were teaching their kids how to swim or play a sport, here I was, representing my country in a far-off land as my wife played the dual roles without any furrow on her face.

Clouded with these thoughts and deeply engrossed in guilt, I never realized when the flight took off. I was jolted back to my senses by Captain Sunil, who shared the disastrous news that our soldiers were served beef by the flight attendant. I immediately inquired from Sunil whether they had already eaten it, to which he said 'yes', and I warned him against sharing this news with anyone. I called for the pilot and explained to him how cows were worshipped in India by a large population. But the problem remained, as now there were very few vegetarian meals available. I instructed Captain Sunil to ask Subedar Fateh to tell our men to eat puri sabzi for the next meal and once again cautioned Sunil to not share this mishap with anyone.

It was a long flight of around sixteen hours, which ultimately took more time than expected due to a very long refuelling halt. We were to halt for refuelling in Khartoum, the capital of Sudan. Unfortunately, we landed there well past midnight only to be welcomed by the airport personnel informing that refuelling could happen only at first light, and since we were a military aircraft, none of us were allowed to deboard the plane. The aircraft was parked next to the refuelling station, and the nozzle of the fuel dispenser was our view from the window. I am sure our aircraft could well have set a world record for maximum hours spent at a refuelling station. I recall to date that the person who came for refuelling in the morning simply said, 'We don't work at night.' That statement made me realize that it was imperative to get used to the new environment, the 'African way of working'.

Finally, post the take-off from Khartoum, we were elated to hear the announcement that we were about to land at Lungi. The only international airport in Sierra Leone was in Lungi, a coastal town in the Northern Province. Our advance party had already reached Lungi with heavy equipment, and the tented colony was already ready for our stay. As the aircraft descended towards the runway, we could see the magnificent crescent seashore and the tents pitched against the backdrop of the uncluttered deep-blue sea extending as far as the eyes could view—a dream location indeed. A deep sense of ecstasy gripped us as we registered the fact that this spectacular view would be our company location for the next few days.

I was incredibly delighted to see that the personnel of our advance party had reached right up to the aircraft to receive us, as there were no security personnel at the airport. I was told that no flights other than the United Nations chartered aircraft were landing there. It seemed more like a military airbase. Our personnel unloaded the baggage from the cargo hold area and loaded it on to our vehicles, which were parked right next to the aircraft. I once again confirmed whether this was the only airport in Sierra Leone, and I was told that it was so.

It was difficult to have envisaged a site like this. And now, my most significant cause for concern was who would stamp our passports, as without that we would be termed clandestine immigrants. Naib Subedar Dewan, a Junior Commissioned Officer who had come in the advance party, informed me that he would get all the passports stamped the next day from their immigration office, which was closed on that particular day. I was thankful to the Almighty that our pilot was so competent in his work as there weren't any marshallers at the runway to guide him towards the taxi bay. Anyway, I understood the system and the prevailing situation that had created a turbulent canopy over a rather peaceful nation, which, ironically, had fought a bloody civil war over the last decade. I ordered for a report post arrival, and Captain Sudesh Razora, my Second-in-Command, quickly got everyone to fall in.

A swift check was carried out before I was given an all-OK report. I thanked the pilot and his team for a wonderful flight, and we proceeded towards our camp, which was pretty close to the runway. My God! What a sight it was—crystal clear blue waters, white sand sparkling like diamonds under the blinding sun, and the officers' mess along with the tents acting as a separating funnel between the airport and the sea. The view stood as an apt metaphor for the life of our soldiers—who are a perfect blend of the might of the sky and the tranquillity of the sea.

I decided to look up the Commanding Officer to give him the arrival report. He was in his office tent, which was adjacent to the officers' mess. Colonel Satish was pleased to welcome me and asked me about my first impression of the place, to which I replied with a question, 'Sir, how long are we going to stay here?' He told me that nothing was fixed. Hereafter, our further movement would be cleared by the Force Headquarters, and lucky for us, the Force Commander, Major General V.K. Jetley, was from India. He did hint at least a month-long stay at Lungi and asked us to commence the training after the initial settling-in.

I decided to look up the company location before I went to my tent. It was around a kilometre away and again not very far from the beach where we were putting up. The boys were shifting in their baggage. Subedar Fateh, indicating the bunch of local girls standing rather close to where we were, wasn't pleased with the security arrangement of our company. I understood his concern and asked for a concertina coil wire to be put around our camp.

I asked for the *langar* (kitchen) to be made functional at the earliest and double sentries to be placed on all four corners of our location, with a proper sentry post constructed. While leaving, I asked Subedar Fateh to warn everyone about the prevalence of AIDS in Sierra Leone, as reported in a recent survey. The soldiers were given adequate information about it so as to protect the larger group. Moreover, in my opinion, as AIDS engulfed the country, spreading rapidly through various means, our soldiers, due to their constant interaction with local leaders, could disseminate the same information to the wider community.

After a thorough check of the company arrangements, I moved back to my tent. My whole life was settled in that conical iron structure. The pictures of my wife and kids framed in metal, with 'My Happy Place' engraved on it, adorned my bedside table. My tent would be my home for God knows how long, I thought, and I somehow had to create the magic of home here, with tarpaulin and not concrete, with sand and not tiles, with photos and not people. The infectious cheer of my kids was replaced by the gloomy sound of the sea. The feeling that I was miles and miles away from home was finally sinking in, and with an abundance of memories I slipped into deep slumber.

#3

Lungi

Lungi is a provincial town in Port Loko District of the Northern Province of Sierra Leone. It lies approximately forty miles north of the district capital, Port Loko. In those days, Lungi had a population of around 4000. It was best known for being home to the Lungi International Airport. The sea separates Lungi from Sierra Leone's capital, Freetown.

The ferry service between the two towns seemed the most convenient mode of transport. Some of the best hotels and restaurants were in Lungi. However, there were hardly any tourist activities in those days. Still, there were historical monuments representing the rich cultural heritage of Lungi, which also bore silent witness to tremendous atrocities due to the civil war.

The ancient name of this town was Medina, and the majority of residents followed Islam. One remarkable fact about Sierra Leone is that religion was a matter of faith, and there wasn't a single incident of a riot as a result of communal tension—something that could become a takeaway point for India.

At this picturesque coastal town, the emerald ocean contrasted magnificently with the glistening golden sand, and even the international airport was across a sea estuary from Freetown. You had to go a long way overland, so the quickest and safest way was by ferry or boat. However, today, a bridge connects Lungi and Freetown, making commuting more comfortable and faster than before.

The sharp-featured and medium-built locals were primarily fishermen who supplied their catch to Freetown. The native population was conversant in English, since Sierra Leone was a British colony until 1961. Lungi was part of the government-controlled area, and there wasn't any intense threat of the RUF rebels. Even then, the locals had a lot of stories to share about the RUF and also about the bloodiest attack the year before on Freetown and Lungi, in which thousands of people had lost their lives in Freetown. (Lungi was lucky, since the significant weight of the RUF attack was in Freetown as they intended to capture the capital city.)

After the initial settling-in at Lungi, I started the morning physical fitness training of my company on the beach, where we had the locals as spectators. The local people were friendly and helpful, but they always asked for financial assistance and food from the Blue Beret. Overall, I found Lungi to be nature's masterstroke, endowed with beauty in abundance and a treat to the eye.

We were here as part of the Lomé Peace Agreement, to which the RUF founder and leader, Foday Sankoh, was a signatory. Still, it had two grey areas. Firstly, it didn't have a specified time given for the RUF's disarmament. Secondly, the disarmament process was termed 'voluntary' as per the agreement. Given these two points, the immediate deployment of the UN force, though it had arrived in the country, was inadvertently delayed. I could foresee that our stay in Lungi was going to be a little longer than anticipated. As a result, our Commanding Officer instructed all Company Commanders to focus on preparation for the following task: gathering intelligence about the RUF and training.

Accordingly, I prepared a four-week schedule for intense training, physical fitness and focus on overall preparedness for the task ahead. The battalion was camping in an area next to the airport, while the company was around a kilometre away, which was enough to give me a free hand in organizing my company's training.

I have always been a dyed-in-the-wool fan of physical fitness—it was the top priority as regards the training of a soldier. At Lungi, our day would start at 0500 hours, with an hour-long strenuous endurance exercise session and running on the beach, followed by a dip in the sea. By then, our breakfast would arrive, under the supervision of Subedar Fateh. I doubt if any luxury hotel could compete with our breakfast spread, given the quality and variety of ration we were getting under UN Peacekeeping. There used to be a little break of about half an hour post breakfast, which was followed by weapons training, fieldcraft, tactical lectures, route marches and compulsory patrolling for everyone in the company. We would conclude the rather exhausting day with a swim in the sea, witnessing the unwavering gaze of the setting sun that slowly sank below the horizon—a horizon that seemed to be stitched with a silver line.

There were a total of three platoons in our company, and to sustain the interest of the boys and enhance the competitive spirit, I started organizing inter-platoon competitions. Occasionally, we would also set up 'Company Barakhana' on the beach. Upon learning of our company activities, Colonel Satish decided to join us for beach volleyball to boost the morale of the soldiers. The evening volleyball matches became very popular, with casual betting on the platoon likely to win and the number of spectators going up since, besides football, volleyball was a much-loved sport in Sierra Leone. We ensured that after the match, none of the locals left without having Indian tea.

Gradually, the locals became very fond of us, and a lot of valuable intelligence regarding the RUF deployment, strengths and tactics started trickling in. Despite rigorous training and intense focus on physical fitness, our boys enjoyed the daily routine, which enhanced the voluntary participation by all ranks into our training schedule. I remember our Commanding Officer appreciating our training model; he even asked other Company Commanders to replicate the same model.

After about two weeks of following this schedule, one evening, when I went for my routine company round after the game, I saw a visibly disturbed Subedar Fateh. He confirmed my intuition by saying that there were 2–3 boys of our company who were involved in philandering. I wanted to arrest this trend here itself, and there were multiple options available, including returning these boys to India. But I was more concerned about the ripple effect of this illegal and immoral activity on the honour and reputation of our battalion. So, I had two different options: either to report the matter to the headquarters, or to handle it at my level in such a manner as to put an end to this trend here itself.

I had a long and honest chat with Subedar Fateh, who requested me to take cognizance of the issue at my level and make an example of these boys in a way that, hereafter, nobody could even think of indulging in this sort of licentious behaviour even in their wildest of dreams. Now, the first issue was the confession by these boys before I could proceed with the punishment. Fortunately, Subedar Fateh had shared the names of the few boys who had been witness to this. I called for these boys, and as anticipated, they outrightly denied any wrongdoing in the company. I then handed them their movement orders for going back to India, which I had already prepared. Seeing the orders, they started sobbing, and that was when Subedar Fateh pulled them aside to give them a piece of his mind.

As expected, within a matter of five minutes they returned to my office not only to confess but also to request the hardest punishment possible. My intent behind arresting the ripple effect guided me to make them stand in front of the company and accept that they were guilty before I proceeded with the field punishment as laid down under military law. One positive thing that happened, as a result, was that the company knew that their Company Commander was vigilant enough to know about the covert events taking place. To cap it all, I announced that the next person getting into such nefarious activities would be unceremoniously shunted back to India, and that legal proceedings would be initiated against them when they set foot in the Battalion Headquarters in India. But it must be said that while the Indian contingent was initiating stringent measures against such disgraceful acts, such was not the case with the peacekeepers of other nations.

I once witnessed an aircraft surrounded by local girls and tiny children at the Lungi airport. Upon inquiring, I learnt that the plane was de-inducting the Nigerian soldiers of the ECOMOG, who had been fighting the RUF before the arrival of the UN force. These Nigerian soldiers had been here for the last 3-4 years now. It was time for their departure, and the girls surrounding their aircraft were their 'bush wives' who had come to see them off.

Besides that, I was well aware that the challenges and tasks ahead of us would require seamless integration among the Indian contingent's personnel. We all belonged to the Indian Army, wearing India on our shoulders, carrying the honour of the tricolour in our hearts and in our minds the memories of our fallen brethren who sacrificed themselves for the dignity of our motherland. We were an army that swore allegiance to the Constitution of India and strove to uphold its core values of unity and brotherhood. Hence, our soldiers not pacing forward as one was a matter to be dealt with amicably, as petty regimental issues could in no way be allowed to wither the prestige of our nation in an alien land with an impending task ahead of us.

The orders came in that the battalion was to get deployed in two places, viz. Daru and Kailahun. Kailahun was the most challenging deployment since it was the RUF headquarters and was bang on the border with Liberia towards the western-most point of Sierra Leone. Earlier, Kailahun was part of the Kenyan deployment. Eventually, they declined and, despite his best efforts, the Force Commander General Jetley could not enforce it since the Kenyans gave a written order against the deployment. There were also countries with vested interests in having Sierra Leone as their operational base—they preferred to be deployed in diamond areas only.

So, there were severe deployment issues that the Force Headquarters was battling with, as on the one hand the area of mobilization was changing day after day, on the other, the headquarters had to keep a check on the possibility of illicit activities that might take place in the guise of peacekeeping. Coming back to the integration issue of the Indian contingent and the orders for Kailahun being the area of our deployment. After every other nation's denial, our mobilization process had to begin at the earliest. I was lucky in this, as apart from my company, the other company to be deployed at Kailahun was Major Nair's company, and owing to the bond that Major Nair and I shared, the bonhomie could be ensured in our area of operation. I believe Colonel Satish had well appreciated the importance of the Kailahun region as also the fantastic bond Major Nair and I shared. Therefore, despite the integration of soldiers being a cause for concern, there was no issue regarding the deployments in Kailahun. Today, when I look back, I am more than convinced of the importance of the lateral relationship between leaders or commanders, which trickles down to their units and their men.

The radio communication network of the 5/8 Gorkha Rifles was an absolute hit, as messages were relayed in no time. I found it very useful, and hence, for easy access, I made it imperative for all company appointment holders to be available on a different channel. I ensured efficient communication as through that, further orders could be disseminated and corrected in no time. Hence, by zapping or surfing channels, I could move from the battalion to the company channels, and I also noted that this practice had to be 'taken home' once we got back to India.

While the different companies of the battalion were each gearing up for their move to the allotted areas of deployment, one evening, Major Anil Raman, the Adjutant* of 5/8 Gorkha Rifles, announced that the Republic Day of our nation was

---

* Adjutant is the principal staff officer of the Commanding Officer who disseminates orders of the CO to the battalion and ensures execution of all directives.

approaching. Our Force Commander, General Jetley, wanted to celebrate the day on a grand scale in Freetown, and all battalion officers were to attend the celebrations. Suddenly, there was a rush of enthusiasm in the evening breeze, and the excitement over the idea of a visit to Freetown made us all grin from ear to ear. The event was to take place three days later, and due to scarcity of time, everyone started working out plans. A conference, chaired by Colonel Satish, was also convened to figure out the arrangements that needed to be made.

The Force Headquarters had to fall back on 5/8 Gorkha Rifles for all administrative arrangements, as this was our national event in a foreign land. I was pleasantly surprised to learn about the large Indian diaspora staying in Freetown, who were extended an invitation to the Republic Day event. Major Ramesh Yadav, an intelligence officer, was part of 5/8 Gorkha Rifles as their Public Relations Officer (PRO). He was tasked with the job of ensuring the attendance of everyone of Indian descent residing in Freetown.

Major Yadav and I went to Freetown the very next day, considering the time constraint, to try and contact as many Indian-origin people as possible and request them to attend the event, which was to be graced by the presence of the President of Sierra Leone besides other dignitaries. This was my first trip to Freetown, though Major Yadav had been there on several occasions. There was a UN-chartered ferry that took our white Gypsy across the sea, and from there, we drove down the streets of Freetown. In the United Nations mission, there aren't any assigned drivers. It is expected of everyone to drive their vehicles themselves, and all the vehicles in Sierra Leone had left-hand steering control, which made our Gypsy, with its right-hand control system, stand out.

Major Yadav, being the PRO, had already developed links in Freetown, which came in handy when we were looking to contact people of Indian descent, who seemed to have created a niche for themselves in a foreign nation. On my request, Major Yadav agreed for an advertisement about the forthcoming event in the local newspaper the following day. It was a hard day's work but satisfying nonetheless, as we had left no stone unturned.

Hence, we deserved a glass of beer before we took the ferry back to Lungi. The local restaurant in Freetown had a variety of beers, from Cobra to Hunter, and a 200 ml can cost 3000 leones; it was like getting a bottle of beer in India for Rs 10,000. But irrespective of the cost, we enjoyed our glass of beer and headed back for Lungi.

The Republic Day celebration had to be a grand success. The main thing on which the success of the event depended was the turnout of the Indian diaspora, a problem that we had already addressed pretty well. As anticipated, it was a splendid evening which continued far beyond midnight, and after the President's departure, the merrymaking multiplied manifold. Everyone was in high spirits. It was a first-of-its-kind event in Sierra Leone since our arrival, and everyone had worked earnestly to make the Republic Day celebrations a success.

The Force Commander was present till the end and was very supportive throughout. We had to take the ferry route back to our tents in Lungi, since the stay at Freetown would have stretched our administration. In any case, nobody objected to a night ferry ride post a fantastic party—it was the perfect end to an eventful day. The previous night's celebration was much needed to gear us up for the tasks we had to undertake.

The only thing missing for me in those days was not being able to hear from my wife, owing to the lack of telephone connectivity. During that time, owning a residential telephone was not only a matter of great pride but also a huge luxury that everyone couldn't afford. Moreover, it wasn't an easy task to get a telephone connection. There used to be long waiting periods that we in the army couldn't accept due to the nature of our job, which required frequent postings. Therefore, it was a priority task for me, before I departed from India, to get my family access to a telephone at home. I had deputed the most reliable signal Non-Commissioned Officer (NCO) from my battalion at Babina, to get an out-of-turn connection from the telephone exchange in Jhansi. I had handed over all the requisite letters of urgency concerning my foreign deputation to Havildar Faquir Singh, my Signal NCO, before I left Babina.

The news that the telephone had been installed, shared by my wife in one of her letters, was like music to my ears. I decided to dial the number from the ISD facility available at Lungi airport immediately after my morning prayer. Standing in front of the telephone booth at the airport, dialling those oh-so-precious numbers and waiting for an answer from that transcontinental distance gave me butterflies in my stomach. The telephone ring I heard was like the ringing of bells in a temple where I was eagerly waiting for my prayers to be answered, and my prayer, my soul, my wife did answer the phone. Her melodious 'Hello' made me fall in love with her all over again; it was a moment when the world came to a halt.

In my excitement, I hadn't even calculated the time difference. It was midnight in India, but there she was, energetic as a small child on a happy morning. After that, calling my family on an everyday basis became a part of my routine. As the ISD facility was only available in Lungi, I wanted to utilize it for as long as we were here.

I also made sure that I was writing a letter home almost every alternate day. Thanks to the swift services of 1 Central Base Postal Office (CBPO) of the Indian Army, the letters moved back and forth at a fast pace. Located in New Delhi, 1 CBPO is specially designated for military correspondence to all foreign countries. The charm of receiving a letter has no substitute. Unfortunately, today's generation has somehow missed out on this beautiful experience, which is beyond compare. I still wonder how merely the sight of an envelope was enough to transmit vibrations of joy and how putting the envelope in your pocket could evoke a feel-good experience.

On those afternoons when I received a letter from home, the lunch would suddenly turn delicious, irrespective of the menu. Post lunch, while lying in bed, I would open the envelope, which was a source of the utmost happiness. It's fascinating how, in times when you're away from family, little things can cause euphoria and paint your life with kaleidoscopic hues. They hold considerably more eminence over any other remarkable triumph. In an age when SMSes and tweets have given us the ability to collect our thoughts and transmit them in a quarter of a second, there is no denying that the warm solicitude associated with a handwritten letter has no replacement.

Meanwhile, unofficial inputs, concerning our further movement to the deployment areas, were trickling down. The stay in Lungi had been more than satisfying, and the mere thought of bidding goodbye to the place was becoming unbearable. Lungi also had a special place in our hearts because the road taking us home would pass through this town, which has the only airport in the country. We didn't even realize how the past few weeks had flown past, like a cool breeze, in no time.

Our Battalion Headquarters had given us the warning order for movement. Colonel Satish wanted the entire battalion group to move to Daru, and subsequently, two companies would stage forward to Kailahun. We were currently deployed in the western area and were required to cross the entire country's width to reach the extreme eastern point that is Daru, which was like a jetty, with Guinea to its north and Liberia to its south.

Sierra Leone is divided into four administrative provinces: the Western area, primarily around Freetown—where we were at that moment—and three other regions called the Northern, Eastern and Southern provinces. Back then, each province had several districts that were administered into various chiefdoms headed by a paramount chief called the Papa Giema. The chiefdoms were further divided into sections and then into villages at the bottom of the pyramid.

The capital of the Eastern Province, where we were heading, was Kenema. This region comprised three districts, namely Kenema, Kono and Kailahun. For us, the terrain was also going to change: from the coastal area to the mountainous with intricate jungles. Though it was located at a height of not more than 3000 feet, it was the density of the forest and not the altitude that was the cause of grave distress. The network of roads hadn't been developed to the optimum. The only smooth way to get there was through the road connecting Freetown with Kenema via Boa, and further movement beyond Kenema was again on a poorly maintained road. The Eastern Province was rich in natural resources, including diamonds, and shifting agriculture was practised by the local Mende people.

The total distance to be covered between Lungi and Daru was around 350 km, and considering the fact that the roads for most of the journey up to Kenema were adequately carpeted with concrete, we planned to cover the distance up to Daru in a day.

As per plan, the advance party was to move a day prior, under Lieutenant Colonel Amit Sharma, and I was to take the main body by road, for which a fair amount of briefings and coordination had commenced, considering the number of vehicles. Finally, it was decided that the main body would move in two sections, the first under me and the second under Major Nair. As this was the first convoy movement in Sierra Leone post the civil war, we didn't want to create unnecessary caution among the RUF cadres. We were also instructed to be self-contained for a week. This drill of the Indian Army regarding self-containment is a tested and proven initiative. As events unfold, you would realize that it was imperative to be self-sufficient even if it was just a day-long journey. All the preparations for the impending move were in place, and I was glad that besides the officers of my company, even Major Yadav, the PRO, was part of the convoy.

#4

String of Pearls on the Boulevard

Finally, the 'D-Day' of our movement from Lungi, 1 February 2000, was just a twilight away. Despite the main body moving in two convoys for facilitating control, the number of load-carrying heavy-haul vehicles was twoscore, and hence I realized that it was going to be an outstretched convoy. I passed a strict mandate for the loading of all vehicles to be completed by nightfall of the previous day, and for the vehicles to begin moving at first light on 1 February.

We decided to take the Freetown–Bo–Kenema highway as it was well trodden and correspondingly, route charts were prepared and issued to every vehicle. A conference of all vehicle commanders was organized at dusk, on the eve of the momentous day, post the lining up of vehicles in the sequence of the move.

Serial numbers were written on sheets of paper and pasted on every single vehicle. Captain Sudesh was nominated to follow in the last vehicle, with the recovery conveyance under his command, whereas Captain Sunil was to be with the first vehicle, with instructions not to go 'pedal to the metal' and maintain the speed of 50 km/hr. All preliminaries were in place, and I went for a final stage check of every vehicle and met their drivers and commanders before I hit the sack.

We were to move at first light, and—my God!—witnessing a group of locals who had gathered to bid farewell to us was a sight to behold. Words fail me. The warmth extended by the local community, the folk tunes of the region they hummed for us, would be etched in our hearts for eternity. Filled with gratitude, we bid adieu to Lungi and its residents and embarked on our journey, all vehicles moving in tandem. The sight of ebullient young children running behind my Gypsy made me marvel as to how such a brief stay had sculpted a rooted nexus with the local community. With these musings in my heart, I waved at the locals, whom we kept seeing gathered on the roads till we crossed Lungi.

A ginormous convoy of around fifty white-coloured United Nations vehicles, including the twoscore heavy-duty load carriers, appeared like a string of frosted pearls on a richly picturesque highway. The fleet was to cross the entire breadth of a nation torn by a bloody civil war that had lasted over a decade. I realized that the thunderous cheering by the locals had continued even after we crossed Lungi. We were carrying a ray of hope for the destitute citizens of Sierra Leone, a nation rich in natural resources.

After being on the move for about two hours, we halted for breakfast. I decided the port of call in an open stretch along the road to avoid any built-up area. The view was captivatingly pristine, with the cloudless sky beaming like a diamond, clear and shiny. With verdant plains on either side of the road, it was a sight for sore eyes.

Much to my astonishment, the moment we halted, the local people ploughing the fields gathered around the convoy, and I could discern the slogans, 'Welcome United Nations', that gave us new vigour. After the quick breakfast, I ensured that shakar paras were distributed to the locals before we proceeded further.

As we progressed, I could see a distinct change in the landscape. From the coastal area, we had entered a vast and perfectly level stretch, with lots of undergrowth and trees and distinct regions cleared for paddy cultivation. Throughout the voyage, the radio sets were a great asset, as Captain Sunil in the leading vehicle was able to tip everyone off about impending stumbling blocks, like culverts, bottlenecks and built-up areas during the journey.

I was happy that despite top-notch roads, the youngster in the front vehicle wasn't moving beyond 50 km/hr, and so all were moving together as a convoy. Also, I was satisfied that Captain Sudesh hadn't reported any breakdown. Lucky for us, since we were getting deployed into a new mission, we were in possession of brand-new vehicles.

Things were moving as planned. However, my intuition kept warning me of some untoward incident that might take place, so I ensured rigorous 'convoy discipline'. Major Yadav, the PRO, who had shifted to my vehicle after breakfast, was also in an agreement that the RUF would not permit us to move into their heartland so smoothly. I was driving with Major Yadav in the front seat when I contemplated possible reactions from us in case the RUF stopped our convoy. Both of us agreed that it would be too premature to get into any confrontation with the RUF since it was the beginning of the mission, and our priority should be to complete our deployment on ground.

I was looking for an appropriate location for our lunch stoppage. Finally, we decided to halt before Kenema, since stretching to Kenema would have been too late for lunch. The arduous stretch of our journey was ahead of Kenema, both in terms of the quality of the road as well as the fact that we had set foot in the RUF heartland.

The lunch halt was similar to the one we had had for breakfast, with the locals surrounding us. This time, a small delegation insisted on meeting me, and Subedar Fateh brought them over. They reported RUF atrocities, which was evident looking at the number of amputees accompanying this delegation. I was appalled to see children with their hands cut off. It was very unsettling to hear their life stories full of monstrosities inflicted by the RUF. However, they were delighted to see the UN force, and the senior person in the group wanted to honour me with a garland. The honour bestowed by them in the middle of nowhere further strengthened my conviction to bring stability and normality for the people of the region. Yet again, we distributed food to each of them, and they were elated and shouted slogans against the RUF.

Post lunch, the convoy ventured into Kenema, the capital of the Eastern Province and the second-largest city of Sierra Leone. At first glance, one could make out that it was the trade centre of the country, with shops and markets all around. Kenema had a sizeable Portuguese population. Our convoy was welcomed with a standing ovation—people stood on both sides of the road. We could see 'Diamond Merchant' written on several signboards outside shops in Kenema, which was part of Kono District, the region with the maximum number of diamond mines in the country. The town was an amalgam of prosperity and poverty, with a vast monetary chasm between its rich and poor residents.

Our convoy steered through the entire city, with lots of cheering and beating of drums by the locals. The loud chants of 'Welcome, Welcome' were pleasing to the ear. We replied by waving at the crowd. Since we passed through the city with the convoy moving at a languid speed, the locals came forward to shake hands with us.

We decided against halting in Kenema as we had already taken about half an hour to pass through the city. Finally, we were on the road to Daru. The condition of the road ahead of Kenema was enough to indicate that we were soon going to enter the RUF heartland. The landscape changed from winsome plains to rugged and desolate mountains, tangled forest with thick undergrowth on both sides of the narrow, broken gravel road. We anticipated 2–3 hours' drive through the jungle before we could reach Daru; luckily for us, around the same time was left before sunset, and I wanted to reach Daru before nightfall.

But suddenly, the convoy halted, and Captain Sunil informed me of some sort of barrier ahead. I quickly dismounted and came forward to see a thread attached to two poles, blocking the road, and a gritty, fierce-looking soldier standing with his gun. I asked the soldier who he was and what he was doing there. To date, his words amuse me, 'My name is last order, and the last order for me is you NO, GO.'

I asked Captain Sunil to remove the thread and continue moving forward. Hearing which the soldier made some noise, as if it were a code. Almost instantaneously, we could hear lots of movement from the surrounding trees in the thick jungle. Suddenly, there appeared a section of RUF soldiers. Their commander told Captain Sunil that he could 'No, Go'.

By now, Major Yadav had also reached the leading vehicle. He immediately sensed the situation, took me to one side and reminded me of our discussion about avoiding any sort of skirmish with the RUF until we completed our deployment. I wanted to see their reaction, so I asked Captain Sunil to let the first vehicle move forward, but the RUF soldiers pranced in front of the vehicle. Their commander was very firm in saying that he had no instructions about our movement, so we couldn't go ahead.

I asked my radio operator to make me speak with the Commanding Officer. In no time, I was talking to Colonel Satish, who asked for my assessment of the situation and the options available on the ground. In the army, the analysis of the 'man on the ground' is always honoured. I said we had three options: first, to fight our way through; second, to halt in the jungle for the night since it was getting close to last light; and third, to retreat to Kenema for the night halt and try moving the next day. After taking cognizance of the situation, I recommended the third option. No immediate decision came from Colonel Satish till he could speak to the Force Commander, who initially was in favour of the first option. Ultimately, I think Colonel Satish could convince him about the third option, and here we were facing the mammoth challenge of turning the convoy back on a narrow track in the middle of a thick jungle.

It wasn't easy, but we somehow managed to get back to Kenema much after last light. I decided to camp for the night in an open stretch. Limited tents were pitched, since Subedar Fateh preferred that most soldiers should sleep in the vehicles. Major Yadav pulled my leg saying it seemed that I liked the beauty of Kenema and that was why I immediately recommended option three, of getting back to Kenema. I smiled and said that I now know the rationale behind Major Yadav's recommendation to me!

The following day's newspaper was full of articles about the RUF not allowing movement of the United Nations Peacekeeping contingent into their stronghold of the Kailahun District. The headlines highlighted the fact that the RUF had turned their back on the Lomé Peace Agreement and was creating obstacles in the overall peace process. One odd newspaper had also appreciated the peacekeepers' restraint in not forcing their way into Daru. Overall, we were satisfied with what had been flashed in the paper, and the Battalion Headquarters indicated that I should organize the company into a temporary camp at Kenema, as any further movement could happen only once the orders were received from the Force Headquarters, which might take some time.

I could reasonably apprehend the strategy of not displaying urgency for our movement since now the RUF was on the back foot. I further realized that our initial plan of being self-contained for a week would act like a lifesaver for us in the current scenario.

I decided to look for a suitable location for our camp. Fortunately for me, the Mayor of Kenema visited us and was forthcoming in offering us a local school building with a huge ground for our camp, since the schools were closed for holidays. Our immediate priority was to organize ourselves into a proper camp and establish the langar, so that food could be made available for all. In no time, the tasks were underway.

I decided to visit the city and personally thank the heads of government of the Eastern Provinces through the Mayor. Upon meeting the Mayor, I was informed that the President of Sierra Leone, Ahmad Tejan Kabbah, was in town. The Mayor suggested that he would arrange my meeting with the President that evening, which I agreed to and accordingly, the meeting was fixed. Since the Mayor didn't have access to any form of direct communication with me, he passed the message through the team of military observers of the United Nations who were located in Kenema. The observer team of the UN passed on the message to me through the UN Force Headquarters located in Freetown. As a result, the Force Headquarters started questioning the Battalion Headquarters in Lungi about my agenda behind meeting the President. After a full spiral, the news reached me through the radio channel when a visibly distressed radio operator came running to me with the message that 'CO Saab'* would like to speak to me urgently. For the first time, I heard Colonel Satish in a black mood because of my intent to meet the President without informing the Battalion Headquarters.

I immediately understood the entire confusion. But despite my explanation, I failed to convince Colonel Satish, who was upset with me for a long time after that. The protocol demanded that I go for the meeting once it had been fixed. So I went for this typical courtesy meeting, where the President appreciated our restraint action and assured me that he would take up the matter with the RUF hierarchy. He promised to find a way so that the United Nations peacekeepers could access all areas within the national boundaries of Sierra Leone, including the RUF stronghold.

I was delighted to learn that the President belonged to the Kailahun district; he was from Pendembu, a town between Daru and Kailahun. He wished me luck, and I sincerely thanked him for taking out time from his busy schedule. It was indeed a memorable meeting, an experience that I would cherish for a lifetime, as it was my first interaction with the head of a nation.

---

* Saab: Sir.

However, it came at the cost of annoying my Commanding Officer, which I regret to date.

After the meeting with the President, I started getting lots of visitors, including senior government officials and political leaders of different parties in Kenema. I thought of inviting the top dignitaries over as a gesture of goodwill for our comfortable stay at Kenema, and that was when the idea of inviting them for an Indian dinner at our camp crossed my mind.

We made it a point to offer them Old Monk rum as an Indian specialty before dinner. The dinner was a typical Indian curry, butter chicken, vegetables, tandoori roti and kheer as a dessert. I cannot describe how ecstatic our guests were that evening, and so was I, as I had achieved my aim of extracting pivotal information about the RUF through the informal interactions. I learnt about the RUF guerrilla tactics and how they used terror as a tool of warfare. I further learnt about their areas of deployment and the weapons they used in Sierra Leone. In my opinion, the background work lays the ground for a victorious feat.

Besides our interactions with senior dignitaries of Kenema, Major Yadav and I used to continually venture into the town to feel the local pulse. As part of these reciprocities, we came across a local diamond merchant who explained to us how diamonds had been the root cause of the misery faced by the people of Sierra Leone. We learnt that the RUF, which was initially formed with the noble motive to fight corruption, was lured into diamond smuggling by Liberia. Diamonds were supplied to most developed and prosperous countries around the world through Liberia. As a quid pro quo, the RUF started receiving the most sophisticated weapons and also drugs from nations that were associated with the smuggling of raw diamonds.

The diamond merchant also went on to explain the Nigerian interest in diamonds and how the ECOMOG, a force primarily headed by Nigeria, tried to forcefully control the diamond areas but eventually lost to the RUF since all the mines in Sierra Leone were under RUF control. He was confident that despite the Lomé Peace Agreement, the RUF would not give anyone access to the diamond areas, not even to the United Nations forces. The Government of Sierra Leone tried their best to control the mines over the last decade but with no success.

Diamond was the root cause for the bloodiest civil war that was fought for over a decade in Sierra Leone, where thousands of people had lost their lives, with an equal number of survivors who had lost their limbs. I was shocked to learn how the luminous shine of the diamonds of Africa had diluted the red stains that painted the nation with the brush of barbarity. He further narrated some horrifying stories, which became increasingly tough to swallow, but stated factual nonetheless— he was reiterating the same things shared with us by a delegation which had met us en route to Kenema.

To further utilize my time in Kenema, I decided to visit the United Nations military observers' office in Kenema with an intent to gather maximum information about Kailahun and the RUF. I must explain here that the UN military observers' primary role is to report about the incidents and activities taking place in their area to the UN headquarters. The UN observers do not have weapons and are not geared up to fight. Before the induction of the military contingent, the observer mission gets deployed in the country. Even the Kenema observer group of the UN had been there for almost twelve months now. So, I wanted to harness their expertise and domain knowledge.

Upon arriving, I was received by the head of the observer mission, a Colonel, and after the initial introduction, he took me around their office and living areas. All the observer missions of the UN are self-contained, as there is no administrative support for their cooking or other necessities, and most of the officers of these missions cook on their own. They also lack military assistance to facilitate easy access to the local people into these missions. Each observer mission team is a group of 8–10 officers, from different countries and diverse backgrounds, who work as a cohesive group for one whole year before the turnover could occur. A course-mate of mine, Major R.P. Kalita, was also part of the Kenema observer team, and I was thrilled to meet my brother officer miles away from home.

Thereafter, I was briefed in detail about Kailahun town, where, as I learnt, the first brigade of the RUF, commanded by Colonel Martin, was responsible for the entire Kailahun District. I was told that Colonel Martin was a young lad, thirty years old, and belonged to Liberia. The RUF brigade was further divided into specific areas under various companies, and the RUF company commanders were accountable for their respective areas of responsibility.

Also, since the Sierra Leone military had no presence in those areas, border management with Guinea and Liberia was handled by the RUF. The RUF basked in the comfort of tremendous local support extended to them in Kailahun, and that was how it became their heartland. With easy access to Liberia from Kailahun, it was a region conducive for the rebels, as their illegal supply line from Liberia could run without any intervention from the state or the military. The then President of Liberia, Charles Taylor, and the RUF founder, Foday Sankoh, had worked together as soldiers and shared an intrinsic bond.

Overall, my visit to the observer base was productive. I noted down the crucial information that was provided. During the lunch that followed, I witnessed their outstanding culinary skills. Major Kalita also told me that on that particular day, his duty was to clean the utensils—that was how they divided chores at their base. The day, with the scrumptious lunch, was pretty satisfying. I thanked all the members for their hospitality and left for our camp.

Upon reaching the camp, I finally received the much-awaited message from our Battalion Headquarters to commence our move to Daru the next day. The previous four days we had spent in Kenema were like a blessing in disguise, since I had managed to gather a plethora of valuable intelligence that would assist me in my task ahead.

I immediately passed instructions for our move and could witness the smiling faces of our soldiers who had been wondering for the last four days about the future course of action. Again, the winding up of the camp started, with the loading of non-essentials first and the balance of the camp loaded post-dinner. As per ritual, packed breakfast and lunch for the following day were prepared in the morning before the commencement of the move. I must share that the night before any movement, the langar hardly sleeps, as after winding up the dinner preparations, it starts preparing for the next day's breakfast and lunch.

On our final evening in Kenema, Major Yadav and I decided to meet the Mayor. Despite our best efforts to refuse, we had to stay back for dinner on his insistence. The Mayor, Christopher Loko, a man of roughly forty-five years, had three wives and was a Christian by faith. He took us through the journey of his life. He told us that he was born in a poor fisherman family in Freetown and went on to narrate how his lust for diamonds brought him to Kenema, a place that played a significant role in shaping his life.

In Kenema, he went on to join the Civil Defence Force when the clash between the government forces and the RUF began. The Civil Defence Force was constituted by the government to defend Kenema, and he mentioned how their force could push back the RUF for over two years. Ultimately, the RUF, which was a force to be reckoned with, made them surrender in their territory of combat. As a result, he was made a hostage by the RUF and later released as part of the peace initiative of President Ahmad Tejan Kabbah, who had a mass appeal even in the RUF camps. This incident brought Christopher close to Ahmad Tejan Kabbah. When Dr Kabbah became the President, he nominated Christopher as the Mayor of Kenema.

Our respect for the Mayor increased manifold on learning that he had fought the most deadly civil war against the RUF rebels. That evening, we bore witness to a very emotional side of the Mayor's personality. But due to time constraints, we soon bid him farewell. The final word of advice by the valiant soldier who had fought the RUF to me was that the RUF respects a soldier who stands his ground under adverse conditions.

We were quite late by the time we reached the camp, but I was relieved to get a 'ready to move' report from Subedar Fateh. Upon inquiring about the company's morale, Subedar Fateh replied, '*High hai, saab* (It's high, sir).'

#5

From the Plains of Kenema to the Tangled Forests of Daru

At first light, after the customary prayer and a war cry of 'Bharat Mata Ki Jai', which was a tradition before any move, we commenced our journey. There was grit in the eyes of the soldiers, and the wheels started rolling with a very firm grip. This time, I had placed my vehicle in the lead, with the strong conviction that, come hell or high water, the convoy would not turn back.

I remember the RUF soldier still being there, and the thread still stretched—this was the RUF's bullheadedness. But this time, it wasn't the 'last order' but an unfamiliar face, who, seeing our convoy approaching, removed the thread and followed the act with an unexpected smart salute. The soldier's salute to the UN Commander was testimony to a turnaround in the prevailing ground situation.

Though the wilderness was becoming dense as we moved ahead and the trail in the wild was in bad shape, we kept rolling forward. I was lost in deep thought about what had transpired in terms of our stay at Kenema, which was undoubtedly a godsend. Being a firm believer in destiny, I thanked the Almighty for putting it in my share of fortune.

The journey from Kenema to Daru took around three hours, and I decided to stop for breakfast midway. At the halt location, I instructed the company for a strict harbour drill, wherein the soldier is in a tactical position to counter enemy action. So, the breakfast halt was a unique one, right in the middle of the matted jungle with sentries guarding all corners. Post breakfast, the convoy moved again, this time only to halt in Daru.

From the time we learnt that our Battalion Headquarters would be located in 'Daru', the name thrilled us, for the word's literal meaning in Hindi is 'country liquor'. We all were looking forward to 'Daru', both kinds. Despite the name, Daru was a very sleepy town, with fewer than 1000 people. The vast majority of people in the town were from the Mende ethnic group. The town was formerly the terminus of a now-closed railway line that used to commence from Freetown.

The only positive thing that we discovered immediately on our arrival was that Daru was home to one of the most extensive military barracks in Sierra Leone. During the British colonial rule, Daru was the forward-most cantonment in the Eastern Province, where a complete battalion used to be deployed. So, the first thing which struck us was that there was no requirement of tents as the accommodation was adequate for everyone, including the stores. The British used to control the areas right up to the Liberian border, including Kailahun, by patrolling.

Moreover, the barracks were massive in size, with high-quality construction. The barracks at Daru were referred to as 'Moa barracks', since they were located on the banks of Moa River. Originating from Liberia, the Moa connects Kailahun with

Daru and flows along the border with Guinea for a fair distance. It is a perennial river that terminates in the Atlantic Ocean and had probably been a means of inland waterways in the past.

Daru assumed importance as a result of its proximity to Kenema, the provincial capital. Back in the day, it used to be the final destination towards the east for all government agencies. It would be correct to say that the actual RUF territory started ahead of Daru. Despite the Lomé Peace Agreement, there was zero presence of any government institution ahead of the Daru jurisdiction.

Nevertheless, Daru did have several NGOs that were operational, and our task was to establish a 'Disarmament, Demobilization and Reintegration' (DDR) camp in Daru. This was the fundamental task of 5/8 Gorkha Rifles, with two companies to safeguard Daru and establish a DDR camp. There were four companies in the battalion, of which my company, along with Major Nair's, were to move forward to Kailahun. The balance two companies were to be deployed at Daru. Hence, it would be imperative to understand that the real challenge lay beyond Daru, towards Kailahun, where the 'jungle raj'* of the RUF was still prevalent as there wasn't any government agency in that region. We could figure out now why the Kenyans had refused to be deployed at Kailahun. However, we were to progress towards Kailahun only once the DDR camps had been set up at Daru. Subsequently, the surrendered RUF soldiers from Kailahun were to be directed towards the DDR camp at Daru, and hence DDR was the primary requirement even for the Kailahun force.

The DDR camps were imperative as all the surrendered rebels of the RUF were to be accommodated in these camps for as long as the entire process of their reintegration and

---

* Lawlessness.

rehabilitation was completed. Rehabilitation of these rebels involved vocational training post laying down weapons to make them fit for a profession like carpentry, masonry, etc. Such training needed time, and the skills had to be imparted as that would be their means of livelihood after bidding goodbye to the bush life. For an RUF soldier, an incentive for laying down weapons was money—somewhere around US$300, which was to be given to them in two instalments of US$150 each. The first instalment of US$150 had to be given immediately on surrender, and the balance was to be given post completion of the rehabilitation training. US$300 was an enormous amount, as it was equal to one million leones, quite enough to entice the rebels. So, a rebel could become a millionaire overnight after laying down arms. This was the RUF's most significant concern, since the money attached was so high that it became increasingly challenging for them to prevent their cadres from defecting.

Furthermore, the government was urging the UN forces to establish DDR camps in order to commence the process of disarmament in the shortest possible time. Setting up a DDR camp was a tough row to hoe. Many government agencies and NGOs had to be involved in the administration process, since both the stay and meals of the surrendered rebels had to be arranged in the camp, along with their training in selected professions. Hence, after the arrival of our Commanding Officer, Colonel Satish, the first conference was convened with matters pertaining to the establishment of the DDR camp.

We had to ensure easy access to the RUF rebels coming from the bush. Therefore, the camp location couldn't be in our garrison and had to be towards the eastern periphery of Daru, as the bush, or the territory of the RUF, commenced from that side. That being the case, an area was earmarked, and subsequent work for the setting up of shelters began on a war footing.

Here, I must state that the pace at which the UN could mobilize resources through the aerial route was commendable. Helicopters brought in not only construction material for the shelters that had to be erected but also carried our infantry combat vehicles, BMPs,* in an under-slung mode. In the twinkling of an eye, the DDR camp was visible on the ground, which had been entirely barren a few days back. Also, we pitched our tents to further reinforce the shortage of shelters, and in a fortnight, the DDR camp was set up. Simultaneously, we were also working on the management aspect of this camp, especially concerning documentation and other administrative requirements.

Daru was like a fence between the DDR camp and the Moa barracks, as we were on the western front of the town, and hence, the management of the DDR camp being stationed on the opposite end of Daru was not feasible. Therefore, around a platoon's strength of boys were to reside in the DDR camp for its routine management.

The health management of the surrendered rebels was another cause for concern for which doctors from the World Health Organization were included in the DDR establishment. In addition to this, the representatives of various NGOs stationed at Daru were on board to manage the administration of the camp, including food for the rebels and subsequently, their training for rehabilitation.

Once all the arrangements were in place, the DDR camp was visited by the Special Representative of the Secretary-General

---

* BMP (Boyevaya Mashina Pekhoty): a Soviet amphibious tracked infantry fighting vehicle.

(SRSG) of the United Nations, who was the head of the entire mission. While the Force Commander looked after the military contingent of the UN, other agencies working on the ground, including the WHO and local NGOs, came directly under the ambit of the SRSG. The SRSG was pleased with the overall arrangements in the DDR camp; more so, with the project's pace.

Other DDR camps were coming up in different parts of Sierra Leone; however, the only DDR camp which was ready to be operational was at Daru. This first camp was also more critical than the others, since it was closest to the RUF heartland, and that was why the SRSG decided to personally visit and oversee the project's progress. The SRSG, while shaking hands with me, remarked, 'Are you the officer who met the President in Kenema?' I promptly replied, 'Yes, sir, it was a courtesy call.' The SRSG smiled, said that he was mighty pleased with the camp set-up and immediately gave the green signal to the camp since the administrative structure was in place. However, our boys, who were an integral part of the management residing in the DDR camp, didn't seem very optimistic about the surrender by the RUF rebels. Some of them told me, 'Saab, UN has invested so much of money in creating this white elephant; however, it is unlikely that the RUF will come on their own to surrender.' I smiled and said in a lighter vein, 'If the RUF soldiers are ready to lose limbs with no yield, they hardly have to walk a few kilometres for a million bucks.'

Patience was the key for us as we had to await their arrival. But I also warned our soldiers to be alert at night. So now, what started was the waiting period for the RUF soldiers to venture out from the bush and lay down weapons at the DDR camp. All means of publicity, including print media and radio, which was a popular means of communication among the RUF cadres, were utilized to announce that Daru's DDR camp was operational.

The wait was unbearable, but in our case, the waiting period was utilized for further improvement of services in the camp. With every passing day, additional refinements, like the DDR camp being fenced with security concertina wires all around, were put in place. One grey area that existed was the mode of payment to the RUF rebels, for which regular reminders were sent to the Force Headquarters. Finally, an official of the government did turn up but only to do the necessary documentation, based on which the government would 'soon' release the funds.

The payment of money, though initiated by the United Nations, had to be coordinated on ground by the Government of Sierra Leone. We were anticipating a severe commotion in case the rebels were not paid immediately after the surrender. But despite the bureaucratic hassles surrounding the camp, we were confident of handling any turbulence resulting due to delay in payment to the rebels.

We waited for a long time. Finally, one silent, gloomy night, the sentry heard some movement in the bush and challenged as per procedure. To his utter surprise, a group of eight soldiers, who had raised their weapons in the air, came out of the dense thicket shouting the words 'surrender, surrender'. The sentry then ordered them to put their weapons on the ground and immediately called for Lieutenant Ankur Banga, the Platoon Commander, on the radio set.

This was the moment that the entire platoon had been eagerly waiting for. All soldiers were quickly on 'stand-to' when the rebels were asked to move inside the camp, leaving their weapons behind. Luckily, both the RUF rebels and the Indian soldiers were on the same proficiency level in English as a language of communication. Each side would speak incomplete sentences at a slow pace.

The RUF soldiers seemed exhausted and famished, and the first thing they asked for was 'chop-chop', a slang used among RUF cadres denoting food. So, first up, they were provided with food. This was followed by a thorough medical check-up, and a stamp was impressed on their hand indicating the date of surrender. Subsequently, the documentation began. It brought a sense of accomplishment and delight among the platoon soldiers in the DDR camp, and on my next visit, I could catch smiling faces exuberant with wild abandon over this feat.

The task of disarmament had commenced, and we were overjoyed since the exercise had started with the Indian contingent being the trailblazers in the process of demilitarizing the rebel forces. However, this posed the colossal challenge of managing the surrendered rebels, which we didn't anticipate would be such a grave concern. These rebels had been fighting for over a decade in the bush. As a result, severe psychological issues started surfacing immediately post their surrender. The situation was aggravated by their violent streak, which one could sense as they hadn't received the money right after entering the camp.

They were accommodated in barracks. It was a herculean task to manage their internal fights over trivial issues. Even their hygiene was a cause for concern for all of us. They were used to the rustic lifestyle that invited several life-threatening diseases, which could also affect our soldiers. This newfangled lifestyle of the barracks was also contested by them, and consequently, they would pick fights with our soldiers on duty for no apparent reason.

I remember Lt Ankur Banga telling me that the most significant challenge was to make them follow a routine, as their lifestyle choices were not really disciplined, by virtue of their stay in the bush. Gradually, the number of RUF soldiers who came to the camp to surrender began to rise; nonetheless, the pace was slow compared to what we had predicted. Some odd RUF soldier would come in every night to the DDR camp, citing the same reason, that they were disgruntled with the RUF as it was entirely antagonistic to what they had anticipated. The frustration of the rebels within the RUF was soaring like a volcano on the brink of eruption. All the rebels wanted money as soon as they surrendered their weapons, but this wasn't forthcoming from the Government of Sierra Leone, and as a result, the rebels were at daggers drawn.

Overall, one realized that managing the inmates of the DDR camp was a ceaseless challenge, and each day was unique, with different sets of issues at hand. I appreciated the incredible work being done by the youngest officer of our battalion, Lieutenant Ankur Banga, with hardly six months of service. As a consequence of his ground task, he had suddenly matured much beyond his service.

Every RUF soldier in the DDR camp had faced such terrible experiences as part of the RUF that merely hearing about those incidents was enough to send shivers down our spine. One face among hundreds that stood out was of a young boy named Moomba, who was barely fifteen years of age. He had been forcefully picked up by the RUF from his home in Pendembu almost five years back, and as part of the 'Uniform Presentation' drill, he was forced to shoot a man at a tender age of ten. He was sodomized by RUF soldiers time and again and compelled to do menial jobs in their camps. The child had no option but to accept barbarism as the only way of life. I was told that there were hundreds of child soldiers with the RUF in the Kailahun Brigade alone. Imagine how many children had been deprived of their childhood in the RUF cadres.

There was a corporal of the RUF at our DDR camp named Sese Moba. He had faced the RUF's wrath over some minor administrative glitch and, as a result, was subjected to the 'half-sleeve' punishment by his Company Commander. This was when I learnt about the RUF's strange yet vicious system of 'long-sleeve' and 'half-sleeve' punishment only for minor lapses (for any major failure, there was the death penalty, a punishment universally applicable at all their camps). Half-sleeve punishment meant cutting the left arm in half, and long-sleeve meant chopping off the wrist.

As an organization, the RUF was run by clever heads, who, while inflicting such brutality, didn't compromise on their strength of troops. Hence, both half-sleeve and long-sleeve punishments were only inflicted on the left arm, since the RUF soldiers required their right arm for firing and defending their grounds. Such cruelty was hard to fathom, but once I reached Kailahun, I saw a fair number of RUF soldiers who had their left arms chopped. There were innumerable bloodcurdling tales of barbarity wreaked by the RUF that were known to us, courtesy of the soldiers who had disarmed at the DDR camp in Daru.

Learning about the commencement of disarmament, the RUF was put on the back foot, and false propaganda, about the Indian contingent vehemently disarming the rebels, was initiated by their cadres. Disarmament was a voluntary process as per the Lomé Peace Agreement, and so far, all the soldiers who had surrendered or taken shelter at the DDR camp in Daru had done so of their own accord. To counter the RUF's malicious campaign, we started audio-recording the statements of surrendered RUF soldiers, and this was broadcast on the national radio. As a result, the public opinion was with us. People understood that the UN peacekeepers had no vested interest in forceful disarmament.

The neutrality of a peacekeeper is the backbone of all peacekeeping operations across the world, and there is no question of compromising this basic principle of United Nations Peacekeeping. In any mission of the UN, in any corner of the world, the day neutrality is compromised, I can say with certainty, that would be the beginning of the end of that mission.

Years later, in 2014, while I was attending the Senior Mission Leaders' Course in Tokyo, Japan, this idea of protecting the neutrality of a mission at all costs was reinforced loud and clear. Our instructors advised us that 'appearing neutral' was as important as 'being neutral' when deployed in a United Nations Peacekeeping mission, as the local community would be witness to our actions, and our actions had to express neutrality as strongly as our ethos.

During the establishment of the DDR camp, we were also busy preparing for our next task—a rather pertinent one which, by all means, was full of trials and tribulations. The task analysis suggested that the initial deployment at Kailahun was imperative. After that, we would commence the disarmament of hardcore cadres of the RUF located in Kailahun.

The Kailahun town was sixty kilometres east of Daru. It had a predominantly Muslim population and was one of the country's poorest districts. It was filled mainly with graded hills, but the fundamental issue was the thick, dense forest, with only one jungle track that passed through Pendembu, which was halfway between Daru and Kailahun. The district of Kailahun was subdivided into fourteen chiefdoms, and each chiefdom had a 'Papa Giema' as its head, whose directions were revered by every person residing in his chiefdom.

Post our interaction with the surrendered RUF soldiers at the DDR camp, I learnt that the RUF structure comprised two wings, i.e., the 'political wing' and the 'military wing'. The political wing was headed by RUF founder Foday Sankoh, and the military wing was under the command of Brigadier General Issa Sesay. The political wing had the larger design of contesting elections in the future, post the restoration of peace in Sierra Leone. All chiefs, or Papa Giemas, of various chiefdoms of Kailahun were under the ambit of the political wing of the RUF. Even the military head was accountable to the head of the political wing, which means that Foday Sankoh was the supreme leader of the RUF forces.

The Papa Giemas of all chiefdoms were also very powerful; they controlled the entire population of their chiefdoms, and they had the last word in local matters within their area of authority. Under the Field Commander, there were brigades, and each brigade was assigned a specific area of operation, of which the first RUF brigade controlled the Kailahun district.

Divine intervention was at play since my arrival in Lungi. During my brief stay in Kenema and subsequently in Daru, I had received substantial information, which armed me well for my next assignment. While I was busy analysing the gamut of information that I had garnered, courtesy of the surrendered soldiers, I heard a frantic call from Major Anil Raman, the Adjutant of 5/8 Gorkha Rifles, who usually was as cool as a cucumber. He asked me to reach the Commanding Officer's office at the earliest. On reaching there, I saw Major Nair already seated. Colonel Satish congratulated me as the orders for our move to Kailahun had been received from the Force Headquarters. In this regard, he suggested that we move at the double. 'What about our BMPs?' was my prompt question. The Commanding Officer told me to initially deploy without our BMPs, and said that as and when the air effort was available, they would integrate with the company. Without undue delay, I reached my company and announced the glad tidings, news that everyone had been waiting for. They immediately got on with the last bit of the preparations, since we were to move in two days' time.

On the eve of the big day, while I was busy studying the route charts and chalking out plans to counter the RUF hold peacefully and implement our ultimate aim of disarmament, the words of my wife crossed my mind. She would always tell me that the biggest glory in life is winning hearts as that was equal to conquering territories. That was when I knew that this idea was going to be the foundation for my further actions in Kailahun.

With this in mind, I decided to call my wife through the only satellite phone available at our Battalion Headquarters to share with her the news about my move. But to my utter dismay, I only got a silent response from her. I could discern in her silence a resonating concern and prayers for my safety. Upon my inquiring further, she said that her 'intuition was sensing difficult times ahead', hearing which I comforted her and raised her morale by telling her that my route to reach my beloved in the prevailing state of affairs was through Kailahun, so it was a step forward. Giving myself the reassurance that time flies and that I would soon be in the company of my wife, I composed myself to focus on the tasks ahead. Little did I know at that moment that her intuition was right and that would be my final call before undergoing an 'experience of a lifetime'.

#6

Bonjour: At Guinea Border

5 March 2000

It was the day when we were to commence our move to Kailahun, a day that all of us had been waiting for since we first landed in Lungi. The anticipation and enthusiasm were so high that I don't think anyone in the company had slept the previous night. The last barrier, referred to as the 'bush barrier' by locals, was just 100 metres ahead of our DDR camp. The danger threshold beyond this barrier loomed high, as from here the RUF territory started. Despite having been in the for around a month, none of us ventured beyond the barrier.

On the eve of our move, I picked up my vehicle, accompanied by my buddy, Sepoy Onkar, and started from the Moa barracks, where we were staying. We crossed through Daru town and reached the eastern periphery of the town, where our camp sentry greeted me.

Usually, all United Nations vehicles would halt upon reaching the camp, because the territory beyond was the

RUF-controlled zone, which, if entered without orders, might prove lethal. But that night was different. Tranquillity enveloped the town, and only the sound of our car's grumbling could be heard far and wide. I drove past the camp, ahead of the bush barrier by about 200 metres, and eventually stopped to have a feel of the RUF territory. All this while, my buddy was all agog, as he had no clue what my intention was.

Subedar Fateh was informed that I had crossed the bush barrier, and he followed me in no time. I was fortunate that my men trusted me blindly. Hence, none of them questioned my decision. Upon arrival, I informed Subedar Fateh that the prayer planned in the morning, before the move of the convoy at Moa barracks, would take place at the site where we were standing that night.

The barbarity of the rebels had somewhat shaken the spirit of my soldiers, and this was the perfect way to boost our morale and conviction. Furthermore, the route was long, with a few human roadblocks anticipated on our way, which could only be tackled if the zeal was high. The prayer was more like a supplication to the earth, to relieve it of the pain it had had to withstand for the last decade. It would also serve as a symbol of the beginning of lasting peace and the end of violence in the country. At least that was what we intended. In the morning, our convoy was lined up ahead of the bush barrier.

The prayer was performed as per my instructions, and I could see the confidence on everyone's face. The usually serious Subedar Fateh was also smiling as he understood the intent behind the entire exercise. The trees in the forest were fluttering in sync with the chanting of the mantras,* as though paving the

---

* A word or phrase that is often repeated to express a strong belief.

way for our move. We hollered 'Bharat Mata Ki Jai', and the convoy began to move. I was quite happy that the 'Bharat Mata Ki Jai' chants went on for quite a distance.

The first RUF barrier was encountered after around ten kilometres, in Kuiva. I met the RUF Company Commander, Major Tom Sandy, who was rather fluent in English as he welcomed us into the RUF territory. Major Tom Sandy was a Christian by faith and was considered a liberal commander by the RUF cadres. The RUF's design to organize our first reception by Major Sandy, to showcase the group's liberal face, was well understood by me. I extended thanks to the Company Commander, and our convoy moved further.

As the route progressed, I realized that the forest was getting denser, because of which visibility was restricted even in daylight. Today, when I look back, I feel that the gloomy forest had symbolized the grave times ahead of us, a time filled with turmoil and challenges. Back then, our focus was to reach Kailahun before sundown, as traversing on the narrow, unpaved track was an arduous task even in broad daylight.

The next RUF barrier that we encountered was in Pendembu, the native village of the then President of Sierra Leone, where we halted for breakfast. Pendembu was a relatively large village, with around 100 hutments. It was one of the chiefdoms of Kailahun. The locals gathered to welcome us, but what struck my attention was the fair number of 'long sleeves' and 'half sleeves' in the village. Even the Papa Giema of the village was present there to greet us. To better understand the ground situation, I tried probing a little, to learn about the RUF presence in Pendembu. My querying was not encouraged by Papa Giema, and his reflex reaction made me sense the local strength behind the RUF.

Pendembu, as a village, was like a beggar's battered tin cup, a place submerged in dire poverty, with people dying of starvation and plague, due to lack of resources and inadequate medical facilities. I mentioned to the locals that though the woods around the town were pretty dense, there was no trace of wildlife en route. The prompt reply was 'chop-chop', two words that were sufficient to indicate that the fauna was found on their meal plates and not in the thickets. The upside was that I could discern a glimmer of hope in the eyes of the locals. For them, our arrival was linked to 'development'.

After thanking Papa Giema and his people, the convoy moved towards Kailahun. As we waded through the rugged roads of Sierra Leone, my thoughts kept turning towards Havildar Krishan Kumar and my other boys whom I had to leave behind in Daru, much against my wish, since our primary weapon system, the infantry combat vehicles (BMPs), had to be left in Daru, to be fetched up later, once we had settled down in Kailahun. Their watery eyes, while I departed from Daru, had completely gripped my mind all through the journey up to Kailahun, as I was feeling the weight of responsibility towards the families of my soldiers. I prayed to God to give me strength to help reunite them with their families after the completion of our mandate.

Thinking of their families, I remembered my last conversation with my wife, and the mere thought of not being able to hear her voice say my name for the next couple of months broke my heart. From my wallet, I took out her photograph, which I had wrapped with love and carried along with me. I gazed at her face for a long time; her dreamy brown eyes pierced through my soul, captivating me in a manner that no hypnotist ever could. Looking at her, I harvested the strength to withstand any danger approaching my men and to safely bring back my company home. At that moment, I could feel my wife hold my hand, transmitting all her positivity. Then, I saw a built-up area at a distance, with a lot of concrete houses, guessing that we were approaching our destination, Kailahun.

The first glance at Kailahun was sufficient to give you an impression of a town lacerated by the most brutal war the country bore witness to. It was a town that was once the jewel in the crown for Sierra Leone, due to the enormous number of diamond mines surrounding it. But the diamonds turned into blood-stained weapons and became a symbol of barbarism and vandalism, causing the slaughter of innumerable innocent people. When we first set foot in Kailahun, there was a weird stench in the air that engulfed the whole town like a repulsive blanket. There was a sense of decay in the surroundings, with crumbled buildings marked with bullet holes, craters and cracks. Young children stood on one side of the road shouting 'Pumai', which we were later told meant 'the white man', and this particular term stayed with us. One wondered what they would call an actual white man.

A hundred metres into the town, we reached the Kailahun Square, a crossroads graced by a landmark-sized concrete building, their town hall. Kailahun had around 200–300 houses, and the ruins of the town narrated the tales of a once-flourishing trade centre that became a hub for smuggling. The Kailahun Square had a vast open ground on one side, where we could see a bunch of people. I stopped the convoy to learn that they had gathered to ceremoniously welcome us, the harbingers of peace for them. The people were all spruced up in their dazzling traditional attire, men in long, flowing robes and women carrying dramatic headgear with such grace and pomp that it looked like a festivity. Amid this spectacle, one gentleman stood out for us. He was a well-dressed man in a green robe, authoritative-looking, maybe in his mid-forties. He was introduced by a tall, flabby lady as the Papa Giema of Kailahun. I paid my respects to him, and he, in turn, welcomed us graciously.

He indicated a massive building at one end of the town, which was earmarked for our stay. I was told that it was an abandoned government hospital around 500 metres east from where we were standing. There was no immediate concern regarding our meals, since we were carrying enough packed food to last us till dinner. But the locals did warn me about the acute drinking-water problem, as most of the local water resources were contaminated. I appreciated their concern for my troops and made the announcement immediately to ensure the establishment of a water point at the earliest, which would take care of the requirements of my troops as well as of the residents. I was fortunate enough to be able to provide that kind of commitment to the people, since I was well equipped to establish a water point, and in any case, water was a vital necessity for setting up a camp.

To my surprise, there were deafening cheers by the locals when I made that promise; the intensity of the acclaim was an indicator of the difficult lives they were leading, without basic amenities like water and electricity. I felt a sense of achievement as we had commenced in the right direction, and all my apprehensions about the attitude of the locals vanished. I took it upon me to provide them with this breath of life, water. After thanking Papa Giema and the locals for their warm welcome, we left for the hospital building.

It was a relatively new two-storey building. However, as a result of being in a state of disuse for the last 3–4 years, it required a lot of maintenance work, which had already commenced under the supervision of Subedar Fateh. I instantly called for all the officers and assigned dedicated responsibilities to everyone to begin our ground tasks, with safe drinking water being our priority. I started the security audit of that building. It was a haven because it was away from the town, but it still needed concertina wire fencing all around. Also, proper sentry posts had to be created for safeguarding my men.

Being a concrete structure, the building had its drawbacks as compared to the high ground, which was a raised piece of ground on the other end of Kailahun town, tactically more suited for deployment. However, the administrative requirement weighed heavily in favour of the hospital building for the initial settling-down period. Therefore, we decided to establish the first camp in the hospital building and subsequently shift to the high ground. I instructed Subedar Fateh to ensure double sentries, with loaded machine guns, and set up dual concertina coil spanning a 50-metre radius around the building. The work commenced on a war footing, and all security arrangements were in place before last light.

The detachment of military engineers, which was tasked to examine the feasibility of a water point in Kailahun, returned with the positive news that the old water point near the high ground stood good chances of revival, and they would get on with the work the following day. However, our generator packed up immediately after it was started, and a particular part had to be replaced. I asked Captain Sunil to get in touch with the Adjutant of 5/8 Gorkha Rifles to have the generator spare part sent at the earliest through our fresh ration vehicle from Daru, since our supplies were to be catered from our base at Daru.

So overall, good news regarding the water supply but not so good concerning the power supply, and for that reason, it was a dark and silent night, with only the buzzing of mosquitoes providing some level of entertainment. We realized that the most significant nuisance in Kailahun were the mosquitoes and jungle flies; they came out to play post sundown and were stubborn enough to stay close to us even after our endless attempts to get rid of them. Still, our mosquito nets were a blessing that ensured we had a sound sleep. Kailahun was infested with the worst diseases prevalent in the world. Even years later, the maximum casualties in the world due to the Ebola virus took place in Kailahun.

Before hitting the sack, I went around to check if the security system was in place and asked the sentries to switch on their heavy-duty torches to review their range of visibility. My thoughts overpowered my sleep that night as I wondered what Kailahun had in store for us in the near future. That was when the afternoon scene of clapping and cheering by the locals started replaying in my mind like a broken record. It made me wonder how the issues that seemed so trivial to us—things that we take for granted, things that are a necessity for us but a luxury for them—could generate tremendous happiness for these locals. These people had faced nothing but adversities caused by the civil war for over a decade. There were children born during those trying times who had witnessed nothing except fighting as a normal way of life. They had considered barbarity and atrocity as part and parcel of having been born in this land, which tarnished their blissful, carefree childhood. It made me marvel as to how fortunate our children were to be born in a nation where they witnessed love, belongingness and, above all, where they had the freedom to be just children and nothing else.

That was when I made up my mind to start with an aggressive agenda to win the hearts and minds of the locals before I got on with the RUF disarmament. I felt confident about this place, as in my head, the RUF lifeline in Kailahun was heavily dependent on local support. So, to curtail the RUF cruelty, we first had to unplug this support system. With these thoughts in my mind, I surrendered to a deep slumber.

The next morning, I got up later than usual and remained in bed for some more time. I tried to evolve a final strategy and give structure to my action plan for the first phase of my operation: 'Win the hearts of the locals.' I was well aware that the RUF needed support from the local population in Kailahun. Hence, I decided to target that support base first. I once read somewhere that, 'You can fight a war alone, but you need an army to win it.' So, curbing that army of supporters with emotional diplomacy was of paramount importance.

I got ready quickly, instructed all the officers to settle the camp and headed towards town to meet Papa Giema. He was the right person to approach as he was happy with my focus on making potable drinking water available to the people of Kailahun. I asked him about the other areas we could look at and assured him of my assistance to the locals. He requested medical help, for which I had luckily chalked out a plan in my mind. I promised Papa Giema that our doctor, Major Murali, would spend two hours every day in the town to attend to all the sick cases, hearing which Papa Giema literally jumped off his seat and thanked me most profoundly.

I wanted to replicate Lungi's successful 'volleyball model' at the Kailahun town square and informed Papa Giema about it. To my astonishment, he was a volleyball enthusiast and had been a splendid player in his youth.

So, in a nutshell, everything was advancing on the right path. After that, Papa Giema took me around Kailahun town and talked about how what was once a thriving trade centre was now kneeling in shambles. Sensing the opportune moment, I advocated that peace and normality would be in everyone's best interests, and I was stunned to hear Papa Giema singing the same tune. This was indeed the beginning of a worthy personal equation. Through numerous interactions with the locals while traversing the town, I realized that most of them favoured lasting peace, but none of them was ready to blow the whistle on the RUF.

Papa Giema proudly told everyone that after resolving the drinking-water issue, I was going to send the military doctor to attend to the sick in the town, which helped me achieve my motive to win over the people. We finalized the town square as the venue for the medical camp. We also visited the water point next to the high ground, where our engineers were already on the job, which further deepened Papa Giema's belief in our intentions.

I drove with Papa Giema in the front seat and my driver sitting behind. Papa Giema took me to that flabby lady's house. I was quite amused to know that her name was 'Sister'. She was a warm and friendly person who always wore a smile on her face, a smile that very aptly concealed all her misery. I was shaken when I learnt that she had lost her husband and three children in the civil war, and that now she had nobody in this world that she could call her own. I told her that she should never feel lonesome, as hereafter she would be my sister. She hugged me with tears in her eyes.

To be honest, I was not expecting things to move at such a fast pace in terms of winning hearts and minds. However, I realized that simplicity was ingrained in every person there. It didn't take a lot to win them over, as minor gestures could fill their hearts with love in no time, and their hearts and minds were one. So, if we could manage to win their hearts, we would win over their minds as well, and therefore, the phrase used in the Indian Army, 'to win hearts and minds', was just 'win hearts' so far as Kailahun and the Mende people were concerned.

If I had to win the hearts of the people, I had to think from my heart. Hence, I rephrased my morning action plan from 'Win the hearts of the locals' to 'heart to heart' or 'H to H'. It was a great learning experience for me despite it being just my second day at Kailahun. I bid adieu to Papa Giema, who shook my hand with both his hands and, with a massive grin on his face, referred to me as God's angel sent to Kailahun. After a very satisfying round of the town, I got back and decided to spend the rest of the day sorting out routine administrative issues in our camp.

The next day, at the crack of dawn, I was informed that a lady had come to meet me. I quickly went out to see Sister standing next to our sentry post. She told me that Papa Giema had sent her and that he wanted me to come down to the town hall, if feasible. To which I replied in the affirmative. My mind started racing, trying to decipher the agenda behind the meeting, since even Sister was clueless about the purpose of Papa Giema's invitation.

I immediately got ready and asked Captain Sunil to accompany me to this meeting. At the town hall, I saw Papa Giema, seated with a couple of smartly dressed individuals, engrossed in some serious deliberation. Papa Giema exclaimed that he was elated at my arrival in Kailahun and wanted me to meet Colonel Martin, the RUF Brigade Commander, and

Major Kupoi, the RUF Company Commander, responsible for Kailahun town.

I was caught off guard but collected myself and shook hands with them. Colonel Martin stated that Papa Giema was full of praise for me and that it was on his request that he had come to meet me. I was still trying to regain my composure, as it had all happened pretty fast, and sincerely thanked Colonel Martin for his wonderful gesture. Colonel Martin was a young fellow, of medium height and with short hair, who spoke English quite proficiently. I promptly cautioned myself to talk about everything barring disarmament, as it was crucial to develop a personal rapport before calling out the elephant in the room.

We spent the next half hour discussing topics like the condition of roads leading to Kailahun, about our stay in Lungi, about India and everything under the sun but the main agenda. I learnt that Colonel Martin belonged to Liberia and, despite being young, had tremendous experience of fighting in the bush. There was a particular gentleman with Colonel Martin who was well dressed and appeared to be very astute and intelligent; I later got to know his name was Jonathan. Jonathan was the RUF master strategist in Kailahun, as the RUF had a system of having an intellectual with every Brigade Commander. He appeared to be highly educated, and I later learnt that he had earned a master's degree from a college in Liberia. It was a very sanguine and warm meeting with Colonel Martin, who, before departing, thanked me for my initiative of providing drinking water and medical cover for the people of Kailahun town.

After Colonel Martin left, I thanked Papa Giema for organizing the meeting. He told me that the RUF men were visiting town for routine work, and he thought it would be appropriate to have them see me. Upon inquiring about the

Battalion Commander, I was informed by Papa Giema that several companies were placed directly under the Brigade Commander in the RUF structure, and there was no concept of a Battalion Commander. I discovered this to be a great system—in guerrilla warfare, smaller entities with fewer vertical layers turn out to be a better-managed system.

On my request, Papa Giema agreed to accompany me to our camp, where he was impressed to see how we had transformed the hospital building in no time. We deliberated on several issues over tea. I expressed my desire to start patrolling the area but was not sure how to begin. That was when Papa Giema advised me to take a local guide provided by him. We shared lunch that day, and he was flattered with the Indian hospitality as well as the food, although, before our rendezvous, he had never known that a nation named India existed. When it was time for him to leave, I told him that we had decided to start playing volleyball in the town square that evening onwards, and he was pleased to hear that.

After having set up our agenda points for Kailahun, it was time to reach out to the remote villages surrounding Kailahun town. As part of this exercise, we identified Gelehun, a village of Jawei chiefdom, the last village bordering Liberia. The name Gelehun, in Mende language, means 'where the village stopped'. And rightly so, for there was no other village beyond Gelehun.

We started early as the road leading to Gelehun was appallingly rutted, as though transporting us to an ancient era. At first blush, Gelehun seemed to be pretty backward; even the canvas erected at the village entrance, with Gelehun written on it in faded ink, had sunbeams peeping through the apertures of the ragged fabric—it all yelled destitution. It was as though the people there were living in the Stone Age, with hardly any basic amenities. Famished children looked towards us with hopeful eyes, expecting a grain to satiate their hunger or a drop of water to quench their thirst.

In Gelehun, life expectancy was not beyond forty. Malnutrition and epidemics struck people down frequently, causing grave damage, as most lacked any source of income or medical facility. They paid no heed to the civil war ravaging their country, as they had greater chances of surviving that war compared to the everyday war they fought in their village: a war for basics, a war for a dignified life, a war not for diamonds or jewels but just for surviving another day and watching another sunrise.

The entire sight was so disturbing that Major Nair and I looked at each other and decided to return to the village the next day with humanitarian assistance, which wasn't our mandate as UN peacekeepers but as fellow human beings. After returning to our camp, both of us spoke with our respective companies and explained what we had witnessed to our soldiers. We deliberated upon humanitarian assistance, which was not our charter and had to be undertaken by NGOs and other agencies who could only be deployed once normality in Kailahun was restored. Unfortunately, some of the people of Gelehun wouldn't be able to witness this as it would be too late for them.

I sought my company's opinion regarding the disposal of surplus dry ration, which had accumulated since the time we landed in Lungi, and we were tagging it along with us. Honestly, the ration supply of a military contingent in the United Nations is always more than what they can consume, as they plan for bad-weather days. Fortunately, we had not yet faced such a crisis, because of which the stock kept piling. I wanted my boys to reiterate my thoughts, since it was their ration. I was so proud when every soldier of my company got up and stated that it would be the ultimate service to God Almighty and that there wasn't a better way to utilize our surplus supplies. So ultimately, we decided that both Major Nair and I, along with the doctor and sufficient food supply, would revisit Gelehun the following day.

The villagers, in all probability, were not anticipating that we would keep our word, but when we said we would visit them, we meant business. The moment the villagers saw the truck full of ration hurtling towards them, I saw an expression on their faces that I can't explain; it was as if the sight of the truck had given them a new lease of life. The truck was their oxygen cylinder in a world with no air to breathe; it would be the reason some of them would live to see another day, and this thought made us feel content.

The truck halted right in the middle of the village. Before the locals could charge on to the truck, we made them sit in a row to smoothly distribute the ration to everyone and followed it with a thorough medical check-up by our doctor, who was well equipped with medicines. This was by far the most gratifying day since our arrival in Kailahun, and we wanted to further reinforce the humanitarian assistance activities, spreading them far and wide.

After returning to base, I contacted various NGOs in Daru through our radio set and requested them to push forward rations and medicines to Kailahun. Thereafter, we replicated the Gelehun model of distributing supplies to every border village. Here I must reiterate that humanitarian assistance is not the charter of the military contingent of the United Nations; it happens much later, once peace has been re-established in a distressed area by the military stationed there. After that, in a rather placid environment, NGOs and other agencies step up to provide humanitarian aid.

The real issue on the ground is that the 'five-star accommodation' that NGO reps feel is 'extremely vital' for their job cannot be put together in remote areas cloaked in mayhem, areas which genuinely need philanthropic backing to rise from the ruins. Somehow there exists a discrepancy between the needs of the common people and the requirements of agencies delivering urgent supplies. We, the military contingent, simply bridged this chasm between those who already had all the comforts and those for whom just one meal a day meant comfort. Consequently, the humanitarian aid started reaching the impoverished people in the most peripheral corners of the district. The real goodwill that started pouring in as a result of this revolution initiated from Gelehun is indescribable. Post the Gelehun revolution, the locals started worshipping the Blue Beret. The news about the humanitarian assistance started reaching every nook and cranny of Kailahun District. Even Papa Giema personally visited to compliment the UN contingent after we got back from the fieldwork of dispensing supplies and medicines.

At times, God shows you the path. To be honest, all this was never part of my plan till I reached Gelehun, the sight of which drove me to take up this agenda to provide to the penniless. Overall, I felt there wasn't a better way to win people's hearts than by doing what we had been doing there for a month, and we couldn't have been in a better position then, compared to where we were just thirty days back, when we had first set foot in Kailahun. Things were moving in an orderly manner, with top-notch security arrangements in place and distribution drives moving in full swing.

One fine evening, I was informed that an RUF soldier had approached our sentry post looking for me. I received the message while I was having an informal chat with Major Nair, and both of us immediately stepped out to find a group of soldiers standing 100 metres away from our post. We walked up to them, with our minds racing faster than our steps, only to realize that Colonel Martin had come to see me. My God! He was a big man in the RUF rebel group, and seeing him stand at our doorstep was a signal that we were indeed on the correct path.

Colonel Martin congratulated us on the excellent work of supplying humanitarian aid that our company was involved in. Still, I knew that Colonel Martin wouldn't come for this one-point agenda. So, I requested him to come to our company location; he was initially hesitant but did agree to join in on my insistence. He looked disturbed that evening, and I guessed that maybe things were not going well at his end. So as a friendly gesture, I inquired about the state of affairs in his organization. That was when Colonel Martin shared the news about the Guinean Army transgressing into the territory of their country, and since that incident had taken place in Kailahun District, he was accountable for it.

I asked Colonel Martin if the news was authentic. He told me that it was a tip by a reliable RUF source, but he was yet to confirm it on the ground. I then asked about his course of action, and he mentioned that he would be going the following day, and post verifying the incursion, he would report the matter to his Field Commander, General Issa Sesay. I appreciated the gravity of the situation and considered it to be the appropriate opportunity to win over Colonel Martin, as that might give me a gateway to delve deeper into the RUF cluster. Something immediately came to my mind and brought an instant smile on Colonel Martin's otherwise dreary face: I asked him to embark on a joint field reconnaissance with us. This was probably the main motive behind Colonel Martin's visit; he wouldn't have travelled all that distance just to provide me with the news of the infiltration.

Today, when I look back, I cannot reckon as to how I ended up making that commitment without taking any clearance from my headquarters. At times, your subconscious or intuition guides you and shows you the light. It was the light I had been waiting for. Colonel Martin thanked me profusely, and I asked him to stay back for dinner that evening. After initial reluctance, Colonel Martin agreed, and Major Nair suggested Old Monk as the pre-dinner drink for everyone.

I was delighted to finally see Colonel Martin in high spirits after a stressful evening, and as the hours advanced, there was happiness in the air. What particularly surprised Colonel Martin was that all the Indian soldiers would be staying away from their respective women for the next one year. I asked him how life had been for him so far. That was when he narrated his life story, and we were spellbound to learn of the tormenting situations he had had to face in his life.

He lost his father when he was six and grew up in an orphanage in Monrovia, the capital of Liberia, as his mother had dumped him to marry another man. Life in the orphanage was not a bed of roses; the kids were treated worse than animals. And hence, to escape the torture, he ran away at the age of ten. Thereafter, the next 3–4 years were extremely arduous. He had to plan the source of his next meal while having the current one. He would stay on the streets, trying every occupation from a domestic servant to a factory labourer. But destiny had other plans chalked out for him. He finally came in touch with Charles Taylor, who back then was recruiting soldiers in Liberia to overthrow the government and spread anarchy.

The rebellion in Liberia commenced in 1989, and the following six years, Colonel Martin was constantly fighting in the bush, mastering the art of guerrilla warfare. As a result, he was promoted to the rank of Company Commander. In 1995, a peace deal was signed in Liberia, but there was havoc in his personal life: his wife left him for another soldier. So, he volunteered to shift his base to Sierra Leone, where, after three years of bush fighting as a Company Commander, he was promoted to the rank of Brigade Commander. He was given the responsibility of looking after Kailahun, the district bordering Liberia, on the recommendation of Charles Taylor, who had become the President of Liberia.

Gazing at the sky, Colonel Martin said, 'I hate women.' One could understand his sentiment, considering the life he had lived, the love he had longed for from both his mother and wife, the love that vanished in thin air. In a lighter vein, he said, 'You Indian soldiers are lucky to be staying away from women for the next one year, as women do more harm than good.'

I could grasp the logic behind appointing Colonel Martin as the Brigade Commander of Kailahun since the route to Liberia from Kono District, the hub of diamond mines, passed through Kailahun.

Coming back to the evening, it was a wonderful time. Colonel Martin and I developed a deep personal rapport and could feel an everlasting friendship taking shape. Finally, after dinner, Colonel Martin left with a promise to meet the next day at dawn for our patrolling to the Guinean border.

The morning patrol, for which both Major Nair and I were going, was referred to as 'routine patrolling' in our sitrep to our headquarters, as we didn't have sanction to visit the Guinean border. We intended to strike a balance between the ground necessities and the official restrictions imposed by higher authorities. So we decided to follow the middle path of planning it out as 'routine patrolling'. Colonel Martin reached our company base at sharp six in the morning, and we moved in two vehicles with adequate administrative supplies for the day.

We were to drive up to Lorlu village, which was around 10 km away and the local Company Commander of that area was to receive us. Thereafter, we were to move on foot through dense thicket for another 5 km to reach Keredu village, where the alleged incursion was reported. I drove the leading vehicle, with Colonel Martin in the front seat, guiding me through the twisted roads. En route, we discussed how the Moa River was a natural demarcation between Guinea and Sierra Leone, thereby diminishing the chance of any border-related ambiguity. Colonel Martin pointed out the fact that at several junctions, the Moa stretched out into a number of channels and kept shifting its course. However, he did mention the border pillars, which were placed at every kilometre, and the verification of the border pillar in the disputed area would aid in indicating the actual position of the border.

In an hour, after having discussed the variegated topography of Sierra Leone, we reached Lorlu village, where the Company Commander received us as planned and was mighty delighted to see several soldiers in the Blue Beret. We started through the bush, which was quite dense. All of us put together were around twenty in number, a minuscule size, in case the Guinean Army decided to attack. This made me wonder how we would justify our position to the headquarters if we faced an attack, as for them we were on a 'routine patrol' around the town. And here we were, with the rebel commanders, approaching an international border. We were exactly where we were not supposed to be.

While walking towards Keredu village, I started discussing the further plan of action with Colonel Martin. I convinced him that a much smaller patrol of primarily United Nations soldiers must approach the Guinean border ahead of Keredu. We decided to take along one RUF soldier—Socrates—as our interpreter, to help us communicate with the Guinean soldiers manning the border. Understanding the criticality of the situation, Colonel Martin reluctantly agreed. He decided to stay back in Keredu, which made me realize the faith this man had bestowed upon me in such a short time.

Keredu would hardly qualify as a village. It had around 2–3 huts, where we halted for breakfast, which was in sufficient quantity to take care of everyone. Socrates, our interpreter, could understand English and speak intermediate-level French, the official language of Guinea. At first, Socrates seemed quite agitated over the incursion by the Guinean soldiers, but I calmed him down and asked him to only do the job of an interpreter, nothing less and nothing more.

After breakfast, Major Nair and I, accompanied by four escorts of our company and, not to forget, Socrates, started for the Guinean post. As we drew near, we could make out their post. The moment we were 500 metres away from the periphery, we raised our blue berets in the air. Our hearts were pounding like a train down the track, as this was our first experience of moving into an international boundary without prior notice. We were chanting our prayers and hoping that the bunker ahead of us wouldn't open fire. To make our intentions clear, we started yelling 'UN, UN'. But our attempts were bearing no results.

As we came close to the bunker, we could only see the muzzles of their guns pointing towards us. Their deep-set eyes glared at us through the lens of binoculars. The one-word order 'fire' would have ended our journey of peacekeeping in the depths of the interminable tropical forests of Sierra Leone. If they shoot us, I thought, would we be called infiltrators by the Guinean Army? 'Stop!' I told my mind. I had no time to indulge the pandemonium swirling in my head. I had to get my men out of this muddle at all costs.

In my academy days, my *ustaad* (instructor) once told me, 'All this *ragda* (hardships) and *padhai* (studies) might seem pointless to you now. Still, you never know at what juncture this learning of the academy might save your life.' The words didn't make sense to me then, but on that day at the Guinean border, I realized how true they were. How could I forget my alma mater, the National Defence Academy, Khadakwasla, Pune, where I studied French? On that day, all my French expertise began to resurface in my mind. I started yelling '*Bonjour*'* in a high pitch, and seeing me, Major Nair as well as the other soldiers leaped on the bandwagon with screams of 'Bonjour' echoing through the jungle.

I feel the bonjours did the trick for us, as the Guinean soldier 100 metres ahead of us replied with 'Bonjour', hearing which we heaved a sigh of relief. The reply from the Guinean soldier was like a blessing which immediately released our stress. The Guinean soldier smiled and said something in French which was beyond my comprehension. I guess they

---

* French word for 'hello'.

were cracking jokes on us, as we looked like a bunch of maniacs howling 'Bonjour' in unison, as if it was some sort of battle cry to invoke patriotic sentiment.

Nevertheless, we were alive! And that was when I asked my interpreter, who hadn't been of much use till then, to inform the Guinean soldier that we were a United Nations Peacekeeping patrol on a routine reconnaissance task. I introduced myself and Major Nair while still holding the Blue Beret in the air, to which the soldier smiled and said, 'Welcome.'

The Post Commander was a young officer who saluted us, offered us a glass of water and inquired about our agenda. I informed him that I was a Company Commander of the United Nations Peacekeeping Mission at Kailahun and had approached the Guinean post to verify the border pillar on the ground. The Post Commander was a positive soul, and he started explaining the history of the border along the Moa River before showing us the border pillar on the ground. Sure enough, Socrates started confronting the Post Commander on some issue; seeing his aggressive body language, I literally had to press his hand to stay quiet.

After briefing us, the Post Commander took us to the border pillar, which appeared intact and untouched, with the Guinean post aligned with the pillar. What had actually transpired was that the Moa River in that stretch had changed course that year. As a result, the border post appeared much ahead of the Moa. However, it was in line with the border pillar.

Having satisfied ourselves, we thanked the young Post Commander and started heading back with a great sense of achievement. I still recollect what I mentioned to Major Nair at that moment: 'Fortune favours the brave.' We were fortunate enough to have exchanged greetings in French with the Guinean soldiers using our presence of mind, otherwise we would have been killed.

After getting back to Keredu, I explained everything to Colonel Martin, and I could see that broad smile appearing on his face again. This was the ultimate milestone for our chemistry. Hereafter, a friendship blossomed between Colonel Martin and me. I vividly remember committing to Colonel Martin that in case of any threat, I would be the first to take up arms and fight alongside the RUF to protect the integrity of Kailahun, my place of duty. I remember that day Colonel Martin hugged me, a hug that was warm, affectionate and a symbol of respect from one soldier to another.

#7

Hostages

After leading a patrol to the Guinean border and facing a near-death encounter, the mutual respect and friendship between Colonel Martin and me was on a new high. We met each other more frequently after that day and openly discussed our issues without inhibitions of any sort. We tried to see each other every few days, and each meeting brought us closer. Colonel Martin allowed our ration convoys to move from Daru to Kailahun without any undue interference, and even the frequency of such convoys was not an issue.

The biggest morale-booster in these convoys used to be the mail from India. These letters were our lifeline, our only link with our families. I was overjoyed to receive my birthday greetings from my wife and children. Glaring at my little angel's birthday card, drawn in crayons by her tiny hands, my eyes welled up with tears. It felt like ages since I last saw them, held them, felt them. I missed the moments my son would come running to me with his homework, or my daughter would request me to help her comb her Barbie's hair. I missed submerging my day's stress into the ocean of my wife's lap. I felt motionless even though each day in Kailahun was filled with unexpected turns, but I knew that I wouldn't see her standing at any crossroads. That void was gnawing at me, gradually lowering a veil of gloom over my eyes. Some days, I wished I had the wings of a bird so I could fly to her for evening tea, hold her hand, feel the breeze singing the tunes of our love and fly back for my next day's task. But alas, it wasn't to be. So, the letters were my wings, and each time I received one, it felt like home.

In my next meeting with Colonel Martin, I even showed him the birthday card that my daughter had made for me. Colonel Martin was pleased to learn that my birthday was approaching, and I took a commitment from him to ensure his availability on 16 April. Moreover, he was delighted to hear that the evening volleyball ritual in the town square was crystallizing into a fiesta attended by everyone. Eventually, even the officers from the United Nations observer group in Kailahun started playing with us, besides the locals and the RUF soldiers.

Papa Giema, being an ardent volleyball enthusiast, attended all our evening matches as a spectator, cheering for the team I represented. He particularly appreciated my technique of gameplay at the net—my body language would make it seem I was aiming for a smash, but I would eventually drop the ball down slowly to confuse the opponent. Even Colonel Martin occasionally graced us with his presence at our evening ritual.

Evenings used to be rejuvenating, with an aura of festivity gripping the entire town canopied in the palpable air of enthusiasm. The best times were the post-match hours, when everybody would enjoy Indian tea and snacks like one big family. A few fortunate evenings extended well beyond tea, with all of us dancing to local tunes. To my surprise, Sister used to be the most active on such occasions.

We had managed to establish a harmonious relationship with the people of Kailahun within a brief period. I decided that it was finally time to discuss the elephant in the room, the much-anticipated disarmament, with Colonel Martin at our next meeting as the clock was ticking. At my next meeting with him, I asked Colonel Martin about his views on RUF soldiers' disarmament in Kailahun. He reluctantly remarked, 'Within the ambit of the RUF, not a single leaf flutters without orders from the top.' And I guessed that he was referring to the Field Commander. He also mentioned that he wasn't appreciative of the forced disarmament carried out by the United Nations peacekeepers in certain parts of Sierra Leone, as it wasn't in keeping with the spirit of the Lomé Peace Agreement. However, he did add in a lighter vein that, 'If I ever disarm—I feel it is unlikely—but if it happens, I will hand over my personal weapon to you and nobody else.'

At this point, he inquired about Major Nair, considering he was nowhere to be seen since the last few days. I informed him that as per instructions from our headquarters, he was busy shifting to the high ground in Kailahun, as would I in a few days' time. Colonel Martin was puzzled as he couldn't comprehend the logic behind abandoning a comfortable accommodation like the hospital and moving to the high ground. To which I responded, 'Those are orders from the top.'

Major Kupoi, the Company Commander of the RUF mandated for ensuring the safety of Kailahun town, was for some reason not comfortable with the camaraderie brewing between Colonel Martin and me. Kupoi was a lofty fellow, with features sharper than Colonel Martin's but not as friendly. He was supremely competitive, and despite his best efforts he could never defeat my team in the volleyball matches that he played almost every evening—something that might have deflated his bloated self-esteem.

Kupoi was a local and regarded Colonel Martin with covert animosity, considering the latter was originally from Liberia. Colonel Martin was an astute man who had reached a level that Major Kupoi couldn't climb to. Still, as Colonel Martin had the backing of the then President of Liberia, there wasn't much that Kupoi could do to him.

By virtue of my solidarity with the locals and Papa Giema, who stood like a rock in my support, Major Kupoi could do nothing to me as well, except dwell in the well of envy. As comic relief, I would occasionally say to him, 'Kupoi, your boss is my friend and Papa Giema, my elder brother. So, don't you mess with me, or else my family would rise in revolt.' Kupoi was well aware of the humanitarian assistance extended by our company in Kailahun and of the wave of loyalty extended by the locals, who literally worshipped the Blue Beret. So, we actually didn't have anything to fret about, as we were standing on a strong foundation that we had built brick by brick since our arrival. Consequently, with the blessings of God, things in Kailahun were moving as smoothly as candy floss.

While the situation in Kailahun was as peaceful as an ocean without ripples—due to the enhanced affinity among the United Nations peacekeepers, the RUF and the local population—the situation in other parts of the country was not very encouraging. Daily reports of clashes between the RUF and UN troops, in places like Makeni, were spreading a feeling of discomfort. We had amicably dismissed any revolutionary sentiment that might prove hazardous. It was anticipated that there would be clashes

Major Punia's first phone call to his wife from
Lungi International Airport.

Major Rajpal Punia with the locals of Lungi.

A meal halt between Lungi and Kenema.

Major Rajpal Punia interacting with the President of Sierra
Leone, Ahmad Tejan Kabbah.

Visit to the UN observer group in Kenema.

Colonel Satish and Major Rajpal Punia taking cognizance of the ground situation and atrocities inflicted by the RUF in Daru.

The Special Representative of the Secretary-General (SRSG) of the United Nations visits the DDR camp.

A United Nations helicopter airlifting the Mechanised Infantry BMP in an under-slung mode.

Major Punia with
Foday Saybana Sankoh,
founder of the RUF.
This was the only time
the Indian contingent
saw Sankoh. The man in
a green robe on the left
is Ahmad Tejan Kabbah,
the then President of
Sierra Leone.

Bonhomie between
Major Punia and the
local people of Kailahun.
The kids were especially
fond of him as he would
regularly distribute
sweets among them.

Evening volleyball
session in the town
square area in
Kailahun. Even the
locals attended as
spectators. In the
picture, Major Punia
is seen smashing
the ball into the
opponents' court.

Celebration of peace in Kailahun on the day Major Punia was released from the hostage situation in Geima. In the picture: Sister (*extreme right*), Papa Giema (*second from right*) and Major Punia (*second from left*).

Collection of surplus ration to be distributed to nearby towns and villages.

Visit of Commanding Officer at Kailahun prior to the crisis. (*L to R, seated*): Lt Nitin Chauhan, Capt. Thapa, Capt. Sudesh Razora, Major Rajpal Punia, Col Satish, Major Nair, Major Ramesh Nair, Major Murali, Capt. Prashant Dahiya and Capt. Sunil, along with the JCOs standing at the back.

The joyous Kailahun force, after they reached
Pendembu on 15 July 2000.

An Indian Army truck, painted in red oxide, crossing
the ambush of the RUF during the operation.

Pooja conducted after the successful execution of
Operation Khukri. Seen in the photo: Major Rajpal
Punia and Subedar Fateh.

Weapons of the RUF recovered during Operation Khukri.

The Yudh Seva Medal, awarded
to Major Rajpal Punia by the
President of India.

As part of Operation Khukri, Major
Rajpal Punia was awarded the prestigious
Yudh Seva Medal in 2002, for his
bravery and unwavering courage in
the face of adversity.

War memorial dedicated to Havildar Krishan Kumar, Sena Medal (posthumous), constructed in Daru, Sierra Leone.

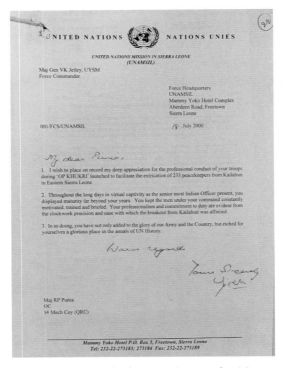

Appreciation letter by the Force Commander, Major General V.K. Jetley, as received by Major Rajpal Punia after the successful execution of Operation Khukri.

between the RUF and UN Forces in Kailahun District as it was the RUF heartland, and that the rest of the country would have smooth sailing for the UN troops. However, the current scenario was the antithesis of the presumption. While we at Kailahun did not push for disarmament right from the moment we first set foot there and thought that winning the hearts of the locals was of paramount importance, the peacekeepers in other parts of the country started pushing hard for disarmament from day one, which resulted in hostilities with the RUF.

The disarmament, as per the Lomé Peace Agreement, was to be voluntary, and by pushing it in the face of RUF troops, the peacekeepers were compromising their neutrality. In my judgement, setting the stage by winning over the local population and putting pressure on the RUF through locals would have been the best approach. In any case, this would not have been difficult in areas, other than Kailahun, where the local people were already against the RUF. This policy was exceedingly difficult to implement in Kailahun, it being the RUF heartland. However, we were successful, and there was an overwhelming sentiment among the locals that the RUF should come forward to respect the Lomé Peace Agreement.

The chief architect of the Lomé Agreement was President Kabbah, and he was from Kailahun. Hence, we started playing this psychological card on the local people. Gradually, it appeared that disarmament in Kailahun would soon be a reality, and even Papa Giema, in his conversation with me, was positive that it would happen. By now, we had generated tremendous goodwill among locals and the RUF, because of our humanitarian approach. It was almost six weeks since we first arrived in Kailahun. We were sitting over phase one's colossal success and did not want to rush things, since any wrong action could have wasted all our hard work. Everyone in Sierra Leone was talking about the success story of the peacekeepers in Kailahun, and it was turning out to be a case study for other peacekeepers.

After this preliminary accomplishment of the initial six weeks of successful deployment in Kailahun, while maintaining peace and harmony along with winning the hearts of the locals and the RUF alike, the pressure was now building up from higher headquarters to commence the process of disarmament. Tales of my bonding with Papa Giema and Colonel Martin were doing the rounds in the corridors of the headquarters. The entire Eastern Province knew about it as well. A couple of articles regarding the exemplary handling of the ground situation by the peacekeepers at Kailahun appeared in the newspapers. A local paper of Eastern Province carried the headline 'Growing camaraderie between RUF Commander and United Nations Commander in the RUF heartland: Kailahun'.

I was in constant touch with Colonel Satish over the radio set. In my last conversation with him, he insisted that I should pressure the RUF leadership to make disarmament a reality in Kailahun. He was well aware of my personal equation with Colonel Martin and motivated me to utilize the bond to turn things our way. I could sense the pressure building on me to facilitate disarmament. Even I was in favour of the RUF commencing at least token disarmament at the earliest.

I discussed the issue with Colonel Martin, who smiled and reassured me that it was only a matter of time and would happen soon. He also shared the news that since the payment of dollars to the surrendered rebels had commenced in the DDR camps, some of his soldiers were more than keen to lay down weapons and start their lives afresh. It was a positive indicator, and it seemed certain that disarmament was just around the corner.

We deliberated more openly on several issues, and Colonel Martin informed me that his Field Commander, General Issa Sesay, was very pleased with the situation prevailing in Kailahun. General Issa was particularly appreciative of my initiative of maintaining harmony and providing humanitarian assistance in Kailahun. I told Colonel Martin, 'Any time your Field Commander decides to come towards Kailahun, I would like to meet him as a courtesy call.'

I remember Colonel Martin criticizing our Force Commander, General Jetley, since, in his opinion, it was on the orders of the Force Commander that disarmament was being forced upon RUF soldiers in areas of Makeni and Magburaka by Kenyan peacekeepers. This meeting with Colonel Martin had taken place after a gap of almost a week, and it was already the end of April. Little did I realize that this would be our final meeting as friends, and that the next time we would meet under totally different circumstances. That evening, Colonel Martin stayed for a long time, and we exchanged views on a lot of topics, including his future plans.

He spoke about his experiences of fighting in the bush since he was a child and how he wanted to eventually lead a peaceful life, probably in America. He was still not convinced whether he should get married. As always, he stood his ground and said, 'I hate women.' He asked me a hypothetical question, 'Major Punia, what if some day you have to choose between duty and friendship, what would you choose?' I understood that he was referring to our friendship. I told him that in India, we were brought up in a manner that led us to believe that even between duty and family, duty comes first. That was why I was in Kailahun. I told him about my last four years of commitment and how I had sacrificed my family life.

I returned the same question to Colonel Martin, who, like always, first smiled and then talked about the stringent protocol in the RUF to follow instructions. The punishment for not following instructions was very severe, which also included the death penalty. I asked him, 'Colonel, how justified are the half- and long-sleeve punishments?' He smiled and asked, 'Don't you have a system of field punishments, even death penalty, for disobeying orders in the field?' He further said that they were fighting a war for the last ten years in Sierra Leone, and there had been many occasions when field punishment was the only option. I was impressed with his knowledge—the death penalty as field punishment existed in most armies the world over. While leaving, Colonel Martin was very sentimental and thanked me most profoundly for whatever I had done since our arrival in Kailahun. He hugged me and wished me good luck and godspeed.

On 2 May 2000, I woke up to a message from Colonel Martin, who communicated to me through Sister that the RUF wanted to discuss modalities for the commencement of disarmament at the town hall at 0900 hours. I immediately spoke to Major Nair, who was at the high ground, and he too confirmed getting the message. This definitely was a piece of good news under prevailing circumstances, since pressure for disarmament in Kailahun was building on us. With a lot of questions in my mind, I got ready and started for the town hall. While leaving, I asked Captain Sunil to accompany me. I usually sought Maa Durga's blessings at our company temple whenever I ventured into town. On that day, however, I was in a hurry and missed out on it.

At the town hall, I was received by Major Kupoi of the RUF, who informed me that Colonel Martin was on his way.

In the meantime, Major Nair too had arrived, and Major Kupoi requested us to be seated in the town hall. We had barely managed to sit on the velvety couch when we heard a bolt from nowhere: both the massive iron gates of the town hall were shut with a big bang. We were startled to see Major Kupoi along with 10–12 unfamiliar faces. They took out differently sized guns, which they had tucked behind their backs, and swiftly pointed them at us.

Major Kupoi's face beamed with a sense of accomplishment, as though he was the cop who had nabbed an absconding criminal. There was a deafening silence in the dome-shaped conference room of the town hall. Then, unexpectedly, Major Kupoi started vociferously charging at me with his words, which had a cascading effect. In a flash, we had a group of armed men yelling at us at the same time. What I could discern from this godforsaken moment was that Major Kupoi was levelling allegations against us, for the killings of their innocent brethren. Kupoi, in particular, also mentioned that our Force Commander, General Jetley, had sent a helicopter gunship to shoot down innocent RUF members in Makeni and Magburaka.

Hearing this, I instantly sensed that there was more to it than met the eye, and hence I tried to pacify Kupoi, but to no avail. He got further enraged, pointing towards 'India' written on our shoulders. One soldier, who was accompanying Kupoi, pointed his gun at me and shouted that their demand was 'Blood for Blood'. I saw the fury of vendetta in his narrow eyes and marks of wrath on his reddening face. Suddenly, the iron door clanged and several RUF soldiers came running, as if the world was collapsing, shouting 'Revenge', with their weapons pointed towards the ceiling. In no time, we were like tricksters at a fair and they, the furious spectators, cordoning us off.

Then, breaking the sunbeams, a distorted shadow entered the town hall.

When I looked up, all my distress evaporated as it was a familiar face. The person was embellished with a rather bizarre ornament. It was Sister, with a rocket launcher strapped on her back, marching towards us. Every step she took made our blood run cold. That moment I told myself, 'Major, you were playing with fire when you made Sister "your sister" without realizing that she was the sister of the RUF!' I shifted my focus from Sister's face to Major Kupoi's irate face, who ordered us to hand over our weapons. I sharply replied that we were peacekeepers and hence did not carry our weapons; I said that the weapons were kept in the camp.

Kupoi then asked one of his soldiers to frisk us, and that was when they recovered a pocket radio set from Captain Sunil, who gave me a perplexed look. 'Captain Sunil, hand over the radio,' I said. I asked Kupoi to hear me out, but he abruptly started shouting, and sensing the gravity of the situation, I kept quiet. I then asked Kupoi the reason for the remand. He narrated the entire incident that had transpired the previous day. The RUF soldiers who were peacefully protesting forceful disarmament by the DDR camp at Makeni were fired upon by Kenyan peacekeepers. Around the same time, a helicopter gunship of the UN had pulled the triggers at the RUF soldiers who had gathered at Magburaka.

In that woeful incident, the RUF had lost twenty soldiers, and as a fallout, they had laid siege to all areas around Sierra Leone where peacekeepers were present, except the capital, Freetown. I inquired about Colonel Martin and was told that we would be taken to him as per orders. I glared at Sister with questioning eyes as she gaped at the tiles on the floor, as though trying to mentally solve a mathematical puzzle—she just couldn't look me in the eyes. She only said that she had no option but to join the RUF after her husband's death. I was oblivious to the fact that she was an RUF rebel. I don't really know the reason for it. Was it that Sister had expertly concealed this fact? Or was it that her innocent face never gave me an inkling about her affiliation?

I had barely processed this bombshell when Major Kupoi and his men took us out of the town hall, where soldiers surrounded each one of us. I was asked by Major Kupoi to sit in the rear of my vehicle, since I was a hostage. I can't explain the expression of my driver, Om Prakash, who was baffled seeing me get into the rear seat of my own vehicle, and almost instantaneously, he was shoved into the driver's seat by an RUF soldier. I was wedged between armed RUF soldiers. The other soldiers hung on to the vehicle from the outside, in a manner that made it increasingly difficult to breathe inside.

The vehicle moved through the jungle track. Major Kupoi, seated in the front, was continually communicating through his radio set in his language. It was a jolting journey, with our heads hitting the roof of the vehicle due to the broken track we were driving on. The soldiers hanging on the sides of the vehicle were continuously shouting, and I was wondering what next. I was particularly worried about my company and tried asking Kupoi about my men's status. He replied, 'The orders for the disarmament of all peacekeepers have been received by us, and no damage to any soldier will happen.'

I told Kupoi instantly, 'However much you try, Indians will not lay down weapons. Every soldier of my company would choose death over surrender.'

He laughed and told me to wait and watch.

After driving for about half an hour through the wilderness, I could see some sort of habitation, which looked like an RUF camp. I got off the vehicle as two RUF soldiers continued pointing their guns at me. Major Nair's vehicle, too, arrived, and he was in a similar state. I saw Jonathan, the RUF intellectual, who came forward to welcome Major Nair and me. Seeing him, I remarked, 'The RUF is playing with fire, the consequences of which will be hazardous. Jonathan, I thought you were smarter than that. I'm amazed to witness how the RUF is on a road of self-destruction.'

He explained that these were the orders from the Field Commander but assured us of ensuring that they would follow protocol. He then said something in the local language to the soldiers who had their guns pointed at us. As a result, they moved a few steps back and put down their weapons. Even Major Kupoi's behaviour changed slightly after Jonathan's arrival. Jonathan explained that it was part of RUF tactics to separate Commanders from their companies and that their next step would be to disarm all peacekeepers as per instructions. I asked Jonathan about Colonel Martin, and he informed me that currently Colonel Martin was in the field and would meet me once he got back. Jonathan also told us that what was happening was a response to the previous day's unfortunate incident in which many RUF soldiers were killed by United Nations peacekeepers.

I wondered why we were not informed of the incident by our own headquarters. Had we known, we probably would not have landed into the RUF trap. After an hour, eleven military observers hailing from different countries were brought in vehicles from Kailahun to the RUF camp, and now Jonathan's major worry was to provide food to everyone. He put forth his concern that the RUF would not be able to offer food to our taste, so he was going to send one of our vehicles to our camp to get food for everyone.

The military observers were petrified; most of them had been manhandled by the RUF. Major Andrew Harrison of England was scared out of his wits. Sierra Leone was an erstwhile British colony, and he anticipated that he would be the first casualty in case the RUF started eliminating us one by one.

The first exercise the RUF carried out was to physically frisk each of us by taking everyone individually into a dark room. All the money the observers had was taken away, and during the frisking, most of them were roughed up. Thereafter, all of us were asked to stay in 'barracks' that had no roof and no walls. Primarily, it was only a stretch of coarse floor in the name of barracks. I instructed my driver to get groundsheets for everyone when he would go to procure our dinner, since it was already well past lunch. The so-called barracks had four armed RUF soldiers on four corners, while the rest went into their living areas.

Major Nair and I wondered what must be transpiring back in our companies. But one good thing that happened was that the food vehicle going to camp eventually got back with all the information about the developments taking place in our camp. Overall, I was feeling miserable, having been separated from my command in a crisis, which is the worst thing that can happen to a soldier. My boys, my men, were my responsibility. But here I was stuck as a hostage without any offence and with barely any knowledge of what my soldiers were going through in Kailahun. I just kept praying for their safety.

Om Prakash, my driver, accompanied by four RUF soldiers, brought our dinner from the camp. He also brought in the situation report of our company being surrounded by the RUF in large numbers. Since morning, they had been trying to coerce and threaten the company to lay down weapons, failing which, they would attack the company. That sight of dead bodies of innocent soldiers piled up wouldn't have been a pleasant one. They also used Captain Sunil as a human shield for terrorizing the company to surrender, threatening to shoot him. I was told Captain Sunil displayed undaunted courage and valour by shouting back at our soldiers, '*Koi bhi hathiyaar nahi daalega chahe yeh mujhe goli hi kyun na maar de. Humare tirange ki izzat kam nahi honi chahiye kisi bhi haal mein* (Even if they shoot me, nobody will surrender, nobody would diminish the honour of our tricolour).' I was so proud of the young officer and wondered where he went right after the town hall incident in the morning.

My driver further shared that almost all peacekeepers of the United Nations deployed in areas other than Kailahun had surrendered to the RUF, and the soldiers who accompanied him were wondering why the Indian peacekeepers were not laying down weapons despite being in the RUF heartland of Kailahun. My driver also informed me that the RUF had captured a United Nations helicopter that was on a routine sortie.

I anticipated more pressure on our camp to surrender since it was a matter of prestige for the RUF. Therefore, I quickly wrote strict directions on a piece of paper: 'No surrender come what may. Vacate the building and dig down into trenches as a company defended locality.' I was particularly apprehensive of my company being in the hospital building since the RUF could bring down the building by fire, thereby causing grave casualties. I gave the note to my driver and asked him to hand it over to Captain Sudesh, who was to officiate as Company Commander in my absence.

That night we lay on our groundsheets, gazing at the twinkling sky, with the RUF soldiers standing over our heads. I don't think anyone slept that night. With eyes fixed to the moon, I wondered how unpredictable life was, where one day we shared dinner with Colonel Martin, the RUF Commander, and the next day we were captured as hostages with our lives at stake. That moment, the hut without the roof was not my concern; the rough land piercing my back through the groundsheet didn't pester me; the angry faces occasionally blocking my view of the moonlit sky was not a worry—all I thought of was my men, whose families were waiting with expectant eyes back in India. I had to take each one of them home safely, but with dignity.

My heart skipped a beat when the faces of my wife and children flashed in front of me. How would my wife lead the rest of her life without me? How different would my kids' lives be without a father? What if I bite the dust here without getting to see them; without hearing my son tell me that he would one day grow up to be like me; without hearing my wife say that she loves me? And my daughter—I was her hero and she, my princess. How would our fairytale progress?

I looked around to see every hostage deep in thought, with uncertainty looming on their faces. There was anxiety in the air, and we decided to discuss the options available to us, as getting disheartened wouldn't help us reach home. All the military observers were confident that things would settle once I met Colonel Martin the following day, as they were well aware of the camaraderie we shared. I distinctly remember Major Suresh Karki of Nepal, who could speak Hindi, requesting me to get him released since he was a patient of hypertension and would die without his medicines. Two more officers could speak Hindi; one was Major Gabri, a military observer from India, and the other, Major Rafique from Pakistan. I was gathering my thoughts as to how best I could argue our case with Colonel Martin the following day.

The next morning, the biggest challenge was the morning ritual. The RUF had created a trench commode in the open for everyone, which began to overflow in no time. So, I decided to go into the thicket but not without my so-called bodyguards, two RUF soldiers keeping an eye on me. You can understand the challenge of easing oneself with two gunmen aiming at you.

Jonathan came in the morning with soap, specially brought from Liberia the night before, and apologized for the hardships that we were facing. I asked him about my meeting with Colonel Martin. He assured me that he would organize it but added that Colonel Martin was not pleased with the Indian peacekeepers not following instructions to surrender. He also informed me that all other peacekeepers had already surrendered and would be released today. Jonathan further mentioned that the RUF eats only once a day, and so our vehicle would only make one trip to our camp.

He warned everyone that the RUF soldiers were instructed to open fire if anyone tried to flee. Then, he reassured the military observers that their belongings and money that was taken away from them during the frisking the previous day would be returned at an appropriate time. Finally, Jonathan left, and during the day, we could see many United Nations load-carrying vehicles, with soldiers crammed together in their undergarments, heading towards Liberia. On inquiring from the RUF soldiers on duty, they mentioned that these were surrendered United Nations peacekeepers being taken to Liberia for their release. The RUF had not only stripped them of their weapons but also their uniforms, which was unacceptable to us

Indians. There was a reason that our camouflage had the Indian tricolour and 'India' pinned to it. We represented a nation of over a billion people, and one surrender would bring down billions of heads in shame. In the Indian Army, even the last breath of a fallen soldier blows towards the tricolour so that it flutters with grace and dignity. Hence, surrender was not an option.

By evening, Jonathan came to call me for a meeting with Colonel Martin, and I instantly left with him. We walked through the RUF camp for around 200 metres to reach the other end. There was a nicely done hut with an RUF flag on top, conspicuous as a result of its stateliness. Jonathan made me sit on a wooden bench and then went inside to call Colonel Martin.

Seeing Colonel Martin, I wished him '*Kai goa ma*', a way of greeting in the Mende language, to which he replied, 'Good evening.' He inquired about my well-being and said, 'Hope our boys were looking after you!' I didn't want to complain about the events that had unfolded over the last two days and instead asked him, 'What next, Colonel Martin?' I knew that had I complained, he would have referred to orders from the top as an answer. I also understood that whatever was happening was a fallout of incidents in Makeni and Magburaka.

As always, he smiled and said, 'My friend, I never thought even in my dreams that one day we would be meeting in a situation like today . . . My sentiments and emotions are absolutely intact, like a good friend. But I am part of a military force fighting for the last ten years for the independence of Sierra Leone from corrupt forces. My organization had great expectations from the United Nations. However, what happened in Makeni and Magburaka was a clear indicator that even the United Nations played into the hands of the same vice-ridden force that we had been fighting.'

I intervened to say, 'Colonel Martin, you bore witness to our work on the ground in Kailahun. Would you hold us accountable for what happened in Makeni and Magburaka?' I further amplified the humanistic approach that I believe in and reminded him of the Guinean border patrol, which I executed at my risk, without my headquarters being aware of it, for the greater RUF cause. Colonel Martin was full of appreciation for our work in Kailahun and attributed our meeting underway to the excellent work carried out by the peacekeepers. Realizing that our discussion was not heading in a direction which could lead to a positive outcome, I repeated my original question, 'What next?'

Colonel Martin said, 'Major, I am not pleased by your company's actions over the last two days.' He spoke about how the peacekeepers of other nations had surrendered to the RUF across the entire country, except for the two Indian companies. He was surprised to see our boys digging trenches and constructing bunkers instead of agreeing to a peaceful surrender.

I explained to Colonel Martin, 'Bud, we Indians worship our guns like God and would rather sacrifice our lives instead of laying down weapons.'

He interrupted me to say, 'But here you are on peacekeeping duty. So how can you compare it to what you do in your own country?'

I tried to clarify, 'I believe that a soldier is a soldier irrespective of his place of duty. Soldiering is our religion, irrespective of our faith, and the weapons are our God. There is no question of us laying down our God.' I requested him not to compare our soldiers with other peacekeepers since we were a regular army that was responsible for the security of our nation, and most other countries in the world send troops that were especially enrolled and equipped only for peacekeeping missions.

Despite all that I had said, he concluded with a warning, 'Brave yourself to face the consequences, Major, as you're challenging the RUF, the most ruthless military force in the world, and that too on our own turf.'

Sensing his style of dissension, I immediately understood the kind of pressure Colonel Martin would be under from his Field Commander, for failing to disarm the United Nations peacekeepers in the RUF heartland of Kailahun. I also sensed an opportunity that might arise out of this pressure on Colonel Martin, and that was the opportunity to meet Papa Giema in Kailahun on the pretext of visiting my company location. So, I instantly put across an offer to Colonel Martin, that I would try and speak to my boys to explore the possibility of reconciliation and sort out the stand-off between the RUF and the Indian peacekeepers. Colonel Martin, with all the confidence he had vested in me over the last two months, immediately directed Jonathan, who had been listening all this while, to allow me to meet my company the next day.

The news of me visiting Kailahun was a source of jubilation for every United Nations representative who was an RUF hostage in Geima. Filled with enthusiasm, Major Nair and other United Nations observers asked me to narrate every detail of my meeting with Colonel Martin and later advised me concerning my future course of action once I reached Kailahun. All this while, my mind was stuck on Papa Giema. He was the only silver lining, for the tremendous respect he commanded among the locals and the RUF. Jonathan passed the necessary instructions regarding my movement to Kailahun to Major Kupoi, and I prayed to God Almighty that Kupoi should not accompany me in the morning. In a little while, our dinner arrived, courtesy of Om Prakash, who also brought in the news that the RUF cordon around our company had been further reinforced.

There was a deep-seated perception in the company that the RUF might attack the hospital location to disarm our company. But I was sure that such an attack would not take place until at least that night, since Colonel Martin would definitely wait for the outcome of my visit to the company, considering how much he trusted me.

Major Nair and I relished the scrumptious dinner from our langar. However, we wondered how difficult it might be for the military observers to adjust to spicy Indian food. Giving rest to my curiosity, I asked the British officer, Major Andrew Harrison, about the food. To my amazement, he replied, 'Dude, in London, I would have to pay at least twenty pounds for Indian curry, which I am enjoying on the house here.'

After dinner, as I lay on the groundsheet, I literally started counting the stars since there was no question of sleep. That was when I remembered my wife's parting words during my last telephone call to her from Daru. She had sensed difficult times ahead, and I marvelled as to how accurate her intuition was. Now, I wondered if the news of my captivity had reached India and how she would take it. I prayed to God to keep this news under wraps, at least for my family.

Another question doing the rounds in my mind was about meeting Papa Giema, as he was my sole beacon of hope under the prevailing circumstances. I did not even realize the time since I was so deeply engrossed in all these thoughts. Soon, I started hearing the routine morning activity in the RUF camp. My thoughts had driven me from the gloomy moonlight to the hopeful sunbeam in a flicker, and I left my groundsheet with optimism running through my veins.

That day, I was the first to commence the morning rituals while all the military observers were still fast asleep. I wore my uniform, and while putting the Indian tricolour on my chest, I remembered Preet, who had catered for individual UN kits for our soldiers back in Delhi. His words to me, that I should keep the Indian flag flying high, stayed with me throughout. That day was a real test, I knew it. Then I recalled the famous quote from my commando course in Belgaum, Karnataka:

'When the going gets tough, the tough get going.'

It inspired me immensely, so much so that I felt a rush of energy inside me. The RUF soldier on duty joked with me, 'Major, I hope you are going to come back. If not, it was lovely meeting you.'

I asked him who was escorting me and learnt that 'Commander' (which was also his name) was the escort Commander. It was an excellent start to a wonderful day since Kupoi was not accompanying me. Commander, who was actually a Section Commander, was a real jovial person. He, along with four RUF soldiers, arrived and shook hands with me in typical RUF style. We boarded the Gypsy to start our journey to Kailahun.

En route, I asked Commander about Kupoi and learnt that he had been sent on a special mission the previous night. I quietly thanked God, as Kupoi would have definitely been an impediment. Commander then inquired, 'Major, do you wish to visit the high ground or the hospital?' I confirmed the hospital location.

In half an hour, we entered Kailahun, which looked absolutely deserted, and Om Prakash drove us straight to our company location. The RUF checkpost outside our company stopped us, and there I saw Sister, who looked relieved on seeing me. I once again thanked God since now I had better chances of meeting Papa Giema through Sister, who inquired about my health. I requested if I could look up Papa Giema after meeting my company. She assured me of her best efforts.

Commander cautioned me to come back, since I was to walk down alone from that RUF checkpost. I started walking towards my company, which was about 200 metres ahead. Every step I took had the bounce of eagerness; I wanted to be confident that my boys were unharmed. They had seen me from a distance, and I heard a loud cheer, filled with gaiety, of 'Bharat Mata Ki Jai'.

In no time, everyone got together and embraced me in a huddle, with Subedar Fateh checking my hands physically to look for any traces of RUF torture. I can't explain the euphoria I felt at meeting my men. I overheard Sepoy Vinod saying, '*Saab, aap aa gaye hain, ab humein koi fikar nahin hai* (Sir, now that you have come, we have nothing to worry about).' That was when I shared the news with them that I would have to go back, and the boys unanimously echoed that they would not let me go.

I explained the entire situation to them and passed certain necessary security instructions. My final command to the company was, 'No surrender come what may'. I spent another twenty minutes checking the bunkers and trenches prepared by the boys. I shared my observations and asked them to improve the overhead protection of bunkers against aerial attack; I also told the boys to lay some obstacles ahead of the bunkers to deter the RUF's move.

Finally, after wishing good luck to each of them, I returned to the RUF checkpost, where Sister shared the news with me that Papa Giema was home. She accompanied me to Papa Giema's residence. He met me with a lot of warmth and asked me about my health. He said that he was sorry for what the RUF was doing, and that was when I thought to myself that reverse psychology was the only way out.

I told Papa Giema, 'Brother, I'm sorry to inform you that my boys have received orders to commence firing from our headquarters. They are further enraged as their Company Commander is held hostage in Geima.' I also informed Papa Giema that our company was equipped with heavy-duty mortars and rocket launchers. I told him that personally, I didn't want war and bloodshed in Kailahun, but I couldn't do anything to stop it since I was returning to Geima.

Papa Giema instantly said, 'You will not go to Geima, and I would not let there be any war in my town. The people have suffered enough in the last decade. You must stay back and stop this.'

I said, 'Papa Giema, I am under RUF orders and have to retreat to their headquarters in Geima before last light.'

Papa Giema asked, 'Do you know who made the RUF? We made the RUF.' He went on to pass instructions to the Commander to send a message to Colonel Martin saying, 'Major Punia is not returning and will be staying in Kailahun.'

#8

Mini Khukri: Gateway Home

Things were advancing as planned, and they couldn't have been any better. On my way back from Papa Giema's residence, Sister informed me that Papa Giema was not delighted with the RUF's action of arresting us as hostages. Furthermore, as a consequence of the humanitarian aid provided by us over the last two months, even the local people from nearby villages, who were a part of his chiefdom, were exerting pressure on Papa Giema for our release. I understood the entire issue in a flash as I contemplated the reason behind this prompt decision taken by Papa Giema. I was glad I had been able to feel the RUF's pulse since the day I first set foot in their heartland. It was now quite evident that their lifeline, local support, was drifting away from them.

This information acquired from Sister, regarding the locals badgering Papa Giema and the RUF for the release of officials taken as hostages in the RUF headquarters, was encouraging. I could instantly sense a window of opportunity for the release of the United Nations observers and Major Nair. I requested Sister for a couple of minutes with her in the town hall before we reached the hospital location. Upon entering the town hall, I expressed my gratitude to Sister and requested that she tie a band made out of my handkerchief cloth on my wrist. I explained to her the Indian tradition of sisters tying rakhis on the wrists of their brothers; the rakhi meant a promise to the sister to protect her forever. She was in tears when I held her hands and assured her that hereafter her safety was my responsibility.

I immediately came to the issue of vital importance, regarding the release of military observers who belonged to powerful countries like England, Russia, etc. I informed Sister that in case they were not released, it would result in disaster for everyone. I also explained to her how the RUF did not understand that they were on a slippery slope, and any retaliatory action from all these mighty nations may spell doomsday for Kailahun. She immediately understood my viewpoint and assured me that she would discuss this with Papa Giema. She then escorted me to the RUF barricade and passed the directions given by Papa Giema to the local RUF post Commander.

And here I was, walking free into our company location. My company could not believe their eyes and ears when I told them that this time I had come for good. There was a wave of celebration, and the company was filled with joy. In the middle of this jubilation, I heard Captain Prashant telling me, 'Sir, now you will not go out.' After the celebration settled down, I explained the outside situation to my boys and said that my moving out of the company was the need of the hour to ensure the release of UN military observers and Major Nair. Captain Prashant volunteered to move out in case it was required. He further reinforced the current need for me to take charge of the company. At that very moment, I did not want to prolong the discussion as that would have suppressed the euphoria of my successful return. So, I agreed to their demand and, as a result, there was happiness all around, with the boys literally carrying me to my command post.

During the evening stand-to, I physically checked each bunker for its range and arc of fire. After rectifying all deficiencies, I realized at last light that all the electric bulbs were concentrated towards the centre of our camp, giving an easy target to the enemy. That was when I got all the lights shifted to the periphery and had them point outwards, to be able to better observe the enemy. Captain Prashant immediately said, 'Sir, this is the difference of experience, and we need you here.'

As a routine, the company was in stand-to throughout the night to drive back any enemy misadventure. The obstacles prepared ahead of each bunker were so made that the enemy— that is, anybody trying to harm our men and material—wouldn't get a free run on to the bunkers. I was elated to see our boys highly motivated despite the prevailing adverse circumstances.

By morning, I made a judgement call to reach out to Papa Giema for the release of the military observers. If I had not moved out, the previous day's communication with Papa Giema would have been understood by him as only a ploy for my release. I could not compromise the confidence Papa Giema had vested in me, and the existing circumstances warranted that I maintain communication with Papa Giema. So, despite the majority company opinion being against it, I ordered Captain Sudesh to continue with our company's charge when I moved out.

After seeking the blessings of Maa Durga, I moved for my mission and was greeted by Sister at the RUF checkpost. Sister took me straight to Papa Giema, who was happy to see me. He exclaimed, 'Watching you stand in front of me today, after your having gone through such tumultuous adventures, my respect for you as a soldier has cut across all limits. I was uncertain that you would return to town from your company.'

I gave my word to Papa Giema that I would be coming to town every day and doing my dual duty of looking after my company and also every member of Kailahun town. I assured him of peace in Kailahun and absolutely no warfare, come what may. Thereafter, I explained the implication of holding the military observers as hostage. They were only observers, without any weapons on them. Hence, if this was widely reported, world opinion would turn against the RUF. Moreover, these observers were from mighty lands like England, Russia, etc. The RUF might draw strong retaliation from these countries. So, I added, in the interest of peace in Kailahun, they should be released.

Papa Giema assured me of his best efforts in ensuring their release, and in response, I thanked him profoundly. I told Papa Giema that I was genuinely concerned for a truce in Kailahun as every resident was like family to me. I said that I would continue to strive for peace even at the cost of my own life. Hearing these words from me, Papa Giema turned emotional. He explained the miseries of warfighting that he had personally faced in the last ten years, including losing both his sons, besides the losses suffered by every home in Kailahun, where howls of grief echoed through the windows of ramshackle houses. Hearing this from Papa Giema, I was speechless and could not hold back tears. I wondered at the strength of this man, who had not shared this with me for the last so many days.

The following day, we received the news that all the military observers and Major Nair had been released. I got to know about it when I came to the town. It was the most terrific start to my day, as my brethren were free from the clutches of the RUF, and

I could empathize with them, having lived in similar abhorrent conditions myself. As a result of some miscommunication in the RUF hierarchy, the military observers, who were supposed to fall back to their accommodation in Kailahun town, also sneaked into the high ground along with Major Nair. The military observers resided with the Indian Army contingent at the high ground for the rest of their time in Kailahun.

Learning about the excellent news, I decided to walk up to the high ground, as by now I had access to all the places in the periphery of Kailahun, courtesy of Papa Giema. Though I had hitherto been unfamiliar to most RUF soldiers, they now recognized me as I walked through the RUF cordon into the high ground, where I met Major Nair. He thanked me with all sincerity and complimented me for the successful release of every single man.

I met all the military observers, who were very appreciative of my actions. Pulling their leg, I said, 'By the way, gentlemen, the RUF wants you to stay in the town and not at the high ground.' It was fun to see their expressions, their faces turning pale as they outrightly declined with a big 'No'.

Major Nair and I discussed the future strategy. We concurred that it was imperative to maintain communication with Papa Giema and to also remain in touch with the locals in town. So, it was decided that while Major Nair continued to stay in the high ground locality and maintain communication with our headquarters, I would have to keep moving out regularly to feel the pulse on the outside. By now, I was anticipating a call from Colonel Martin, and as expected, the moment I stepped out of the high ground, I met Commander, who informed me that Colonel Martin was in town and wanted to have a rendezvous with me.

With apprehensions in my mind, I reached the town hall to meet the Colonel. He looked very disturbed and peeved with me for the events that had transpired over the last seventy-two hours. I explained to Colonel Martin that there was absolutely no possibility of surrender by Indian peacekeepers without a fight between the RUF and the United Nations soldiers. The rest was his call. I also explained once again how an Indian soldier worships his weapon as his God. I assured him that I was his friend yesterday and would continue to be his friend trying to explore an amicable solution to the stand-off. Colonel Martin was very upset about the military observers moving into the high ground and asked me to deploy them outside the town. Knowing fully well that they wouldn't come out, I still said that I would try my best.

Luckily for me, Papa Giema arrived at that very moment, and there was an altercation between Colonel Martin and Papa Giema. They argued with each other in their language for quite some time. Eventually, Colonel Martin left in an animated state without sharing a word with me.

Papa Giema then established that I would have his unconditional support. He mentioned that he had made it very clear to Colonel Martin that if the RUF caused any harm to the Indian peacekeepers, the locals would withdraw their support. I thanked Papa Giema with all my heart and told him that peace would prevail in Kailahun come what may.

After that, I took Papa Giema's permission to get back to the hospital location with a promise to meet the following day. While walking back to the hospital location, I knew that I would have to live up to Papa Giema's expectations and find a solution to the stand-off without bloodshed. I was released because of Papa Giema's sustained efforts. Hence, I owed my life to him, and it was because of him that there was no fear in me whenever I walked outside our camp location.

On all such occasions, I preferred walking rather than using a vehicle, not wanting to risk my driver's life. I didn't know what had happened to me since the time I was taken hostage—I considered myself to be on a mission of my own to restore peace and normality in Kailahun. I was aware that this could happen only if I spoke from a position of strength to Colonel Martin rather than from a position of weakness. This could happen only if our defences were well prepared, and we were absolutely ready to face any catastrophe inflicted by the RUF.

Simultaneously, I would have to explore the feasibility of peace without active warfare by moving out into the town to interact with locals. I was juggling two hats: one of a soldier and commander of a company; and the other of a crusader of peace in Kailahun. It was as if my identity was torn. But to be honest, I surprised myself as I stepped into both shoes with the utmost ease, without making any compromises in either role. I prayed to God to give me the strength to discharge my duty towards both my obligations. Engrossed deep in my thoughts, I did not realize when I reached the camp.

Upon reaching the company location, I was informed that my Commanding Officer, Colonel Satish, wanted to speak to me. I headed for the radio room right away. The Colonel initially complimented me for ensuring the release of all peacekeepers, including the military observers. He then told me about an unfortunate incident: our Second-in-Command, Lieutenant Colonel Amit Sharma, and his patrol had been taken hostage by the RUF at Kuiva, around 10 km from Daru. He said that Lieutenant Colonel Amit Sharma had started for Kailahun to resolve the crisis and was held hostage along with his party en route. He also assured me of prudent diplomacy at the highest level to find an amicable solution to the prevailing situation as the issue had been raised in the Indian parliament. Prime Minister Atal Bihari Vajpayee had spoken to his Liberian counterpart, Charles Taylor, asking him to direct the RUF for the release of Indian peacekeepers in Kailahun.

The issue was being taken up by the Indian representatives to the United Nations headquarters for a prompt solution. Colonel Satish once again directed me not to venture out of our company locality since everyone at Kailahun had been released. I requested that I should be allowed to use my discretion for such decisions, since I was the man on the ground.

After the lengthy conversation with our Commanding Officer, I called for all our Company Officers to brief them regarding the current situation outside our four walls, and to coordinate other operational and immediate administrative issues. I told them that this was going to be a long battle. We would have to keep our soldiers motivated. My immediate concern was the stock of rations that needed to be scaled to sustain for a while. Despite the best efforts to resolve the impasse through diplomacy, both at the highest and ground levels, we needed to be prepared for all contingencies. I instructed Captain Prashant to select the twenty finest boys of our company to form a 'Ghatak Platoon', in case there arose a need for a special task as a retaliatory measure to an assault by the RUF. The platoon should be prepared to undertake special operations, including commando tasks, and their training under him must commence from the following day.

The company continued to be in stand-to for the entire night, with soldiers resting in shifts during the day. In the end, I instructed Subedar Fateh to confirm by next morning how long we could sustain with the current stock of ration. The most disturbing news was shared by Captain Sudesh, who had spoken to our Operations Officer at Daru. Captain Sudesh learnt that, as a result of the ongoing crisis and the likelihood of the RUF attacking Freetown, the Force Headquarters was winding up to return home. I smiled and told my officers that we had only two options—to either go back with our honour and respect stripped off or fight to the last man, last round.

The moment the conference was over, I was struck with the thought that since the hostage issue had been raised in the Indian parliament, my wife would be well aware of the ill-fated developments. The mere thought gave me a sinking feeling, as there was no way we could communicate home. However, my duty and responsibility as Company Commander brought me back into my element. During the stand-to at night, I moved from bunker to bunker as this was an opportunity to meet every boy of our company. I would fail in my duty if I don't share here that every soldier seemed highly motivated and expressed to me that he was ready to die rather than lay down his weapons. Such prowess is among the reasons that the Indian Army is a cut above the rest.

The stalemate in the ground situation continued, and I kept discharging my duties as the Company Commander at night. We were in a state of high alert, with ammunition loaded into our weapons. The soldiers kept a vigilant eye out for any sign of trouble all through the night. Nobody slept at night in our area. I moved out to the town during the day to sense the developments on the other side. There was a sense of fear setting in among the locals. They were getting more and more convinced that war was inevitable, though I was optimistic that high-level diplomacy would solve the ongoing stand-off.

Therefore, the best option under these circumstances was to stand firm and show no visible sign of any weakness, despite the limited stocks of ration which we had scaled. To my surprise, even though one meal a day was available for everyone, some of our boys were not eating at all. That's what stress can do to individuals. One fine morning, Major Murali, our doctor, came to me with information about an urgent surgery required to save the life of one of our boys. Sepoy Jayjeet had not passed stool for the last ten days. His stomach had swelled up like a balloon, and it was suspected to be a case of intestine twist. The only remedy was an urgent surgery. Major Murali explained that it probably happened as a result of severe stress and that Sepoy Jayjeet needed immediate air evacuation or he may not survive. He was to be evacuated to Daru, where a field hospital had been set up and a specialist surgeon was available. I was in a dilemma as our entire company was under the RUF cordon, with no possibility of an evacuation. So, I decided to discuss the issue with Papa Giema.

Before moving out, I called for my officers to discuss the broader issue of combating stress. All of us unanimously agreed to follow a set routine during the day, including training, physical activity and a friendly game of volleyball in the evening to keep our men occupied. I passed executive orders for it, and the earlier approach of allowing rest during daytime was changed to routine activity throughout the day.

Papa Giema displayed tremendous concern for my soldier. However, he conveyed his inability to facilitate the air evacuation since it was within the military's purview and only Colonel Martin could take a call on it. Without any further ado, I called for an immediate flag meeting with Colonel Martin. The message was sent through the person in charge of the RUF's communications wing. Colonel Martin immediately responded to my call, perhaps sensing a possibility that he could make us lay down our weapons.

That evening, we met in the town hall, after almost a fortnight. He looked exhausted, and from him I learnt that the prevailing situation in other parts of the country was likely to again escalate into a full-fledged civil war. This time he appeared a little mellow and posed a question to me: 'Major, how long will you continue in the present state without any rations and food supply?' I could sense a shift in his strategy, from an earlier emphatic approach to force us to lay down weapons immediately, even by coercion, to a wait-and-watch policy.

I thought it to be the right opportunity and requested him to help save the life of my soldier by allowing an air evacuation on humanitarian grounds. Major Kupoi, who accompanied him, immediately declined my request and said, 'No helicopter gunship.' He warned me that they would shoot down the helicopter if it entered their territory. I could understand Kupoi's reaction. The RUF had suffered multiple casualties during the civil war from machine guns mounted on helicopters. I again appealed to Colonel Martin and explained the urgency of taking my soldier to Daru, where a surgeon was available to handle the case.

Colonel Martin went quiet, and spoke after a minute. He asked me to provide a vehicle so that the casualty could be transported by road. This time, it was my turn to go quiet, but my soldier's life was more valuable than the cost of a machine. Hence, I agreed to provide a vehicle but insisted that it be driven by the RUF as I did not want to risk another soldier's life by sending him along. The RUF, being their typical selves, never returned my vehicle, though we recovered it during Operation Khukri on 15 July 2000.

I thanked Colonel Martin for the humanitarian gesture and requested for more such flag meetings to ensure peace in Kailahun. I once again assured him of my commitment to peace in Kailahun in the true spirit of a peacekeeper. I was also particularly delighted since he had not raised the issue of our relinquishing our weapons to the RUF.

With each passing day, the graph of my confidence in a diplomatic solution was going down, even as the stress level on the ground, despite our best efforts, shot up. The remaining ration at the hospital location could only ensure our sustenance for another ten days. However, the situation at the high ground was slightly better since the amount of food there was more than our requirements, given that both companies were to ultimately shift to the high ground as per the earlier plan.

I was continually going through the night's stand-to routine and moving to town by day while also attending the occasional flag meeting with Colonel Martin, whose smile was intact since he now believed that it was only a matter of time before we laid down our weapons. We had tried our best but now the message from higher headquarters was flickering. We were informed that 'In case the commander on the ground feels that by laying down weapons he can save the lives of his soldiers, he can take his call.' Few words with profound implications.

I understood that high-level diplomacy had failed, and hence action taken on the ground would determine our future. However, the soldier in me was not ready to give up, come rain or shine. The day we donned our revered uniform, owing allegiance to our motherland, that nine-letter contemptible word 'SURRENDER' was off-limits. For us, death is not an outcome to be dreaded, but the idea of surrender is appalling because of what dies inside us while we are still alive. I was utterly grateful that my men felt the same sentiment.

Right then, I could hear Major Nair on the radio set, notifying that the military observers were creating a shedload of inconvenience for him: they were insisting on being allowed to venture out. I decided to personally visit the high ground to meet the military observers the following day.

While trudging through the town, I noticed the locals, their faces marked with terror, reinforcing their houses with earthwork to enhance the protection of the front walls. Upon approaching the high ground, Major Nair told me about the mercurial attitude of the military observers, who were initially too petrified to move out but now desired to leave the locality and get released through the RUF since they didn't have any weapons on them. He informed me how Major Andrew Harrison of England and the Russian officer had tried eloping one night and were caught by our sentry on duty.

I spoke with all the military observers collectively. I explained to them the criticality of the situation and the strong possibility of the commencement of the civil war in Sierra Leone post the forceful disarmament of UN peacekeepers by the RUF. I further tried to convince them that it was not safe for them to venture out. But they insisted on being allowed to move out as they didn't have any weapons on them, and so the stand-off between the Indian peacekeepers and the RUF, who wanted the peacekeepers to lay down arms, did not apply to them. I once again made it clear to them that they were responsible for their safety until the time they were residing in the town, but now that they had entered the high ground, safeguarding their lives was our responsibility.

I requested Major Nair to put a guard as a measure of protection and informed them that they were not going anywhere. Major Andrew Harrison tried to threaten me; he warned me that he would take up the issue with the UN Headquarters as and when he was released.

Before setting out for my location, I explained to Major Nair, confidentially, that if the military observers were allowed to leave, the world would forget about us, and he understood this from the right perspective. I also informed Major Nair that I was looking for a window of opportunity to join him in the high ground since administratively, I couldn't sustain at the hospital location beyond a week. Furthermore, the hospital location was not very safe compared to the high ground, and also, if both the companies integrated their strengths on the ground, the impact would increase manifold.

Every time I walked out of the company location to move into town, our sentry on duty would wish me in a manner that meant he was praying for my safe return. Similarly, whenever I walked back into the company, the sentry's eyes seemed to chant prayers to thank God as he could see me again. He would try to read my expression for some signs of glad tidings which I might be bringing in from the town regarding the resolution of this impasse. I had also made it a routine to seek Maa Durga's blessings at our company temple while moving in or out, without fail.

The situation was getting tense by the day, with no signs of an immediate solution to the stand-off. A month had passed. I thought about the feasibility of shifting from the hospital location to the high ground and drew up an optimal plan.

I saw a glimmer of hope when Papa Giema informed me of a crisis brewing up in Liberia. As a result, Colonel Martin might direct some RUF troops from Kailahun to Liberia to address the issue. After receiving this input, I asked my platoons to be on the lookout for any change in the RUF deployment around our company location.

One particular incident that confirmed the input of Papa Giema was when, through the southern edge of the bush, a couple of children managed to reach our forward post to deliver papayas plucked from the jungle for our boys. We were absolutely moved by this gesture since it was a testament to the goodwill we had earned among the locals. It was ironic how people in Kailahun were dying of hunger when papayas—or po-po, as they would call them—grew in abundance in the wild. The locals didn't think of po-po as food, but as we soldiers relished it, they would pluck some for us.

I sent out a patrol under the command of Captain Prashant at nightfall the following day, to verify the presence of the RUF soldiers towards the southern side of the jungle. Our boys could go right up to the high ground, which was just around one kilometre away, through the forest. They returned to share the positive news of no RUF presence. This was the golden opportunity I had been waiting for. The RUF had checkposts on all tracks leading out of our locality, but the southern extremity of the bush was not manned.

Most of our heavy vehicles had already been parked in the high ground before the crisis and we only had two light vehicles with us, of which we had given one to the RUF for the evacuation of Sepoy Jayjeet. Basically, what was left was my vehicle, which I decided to use while going to the town and the high ground the next day. The following day, I parked my vehicle in the high ground and reached my company on foot. Then, we drafted a strategy to proceed in a trickle method over two nights through the dense thicket and carry the essential stores manually. I was taking an enormous risk, but under prevailing circumstances, any alternative would have led to serious problems: we could either have died of starvation or chosen to fight it out.

According to the plan of action, the Ghatak Platoon and Motorized Platoon were to leapfrog on the first night, that too in the trickle method of not more than a section (ten soldiers) at one time, and there had to be a gap of ten minutes between two sections. The men moved as swiftly as the wind; they were like ghosts traversing through the triple-canopy jungle terrain that was as silent as the grave.

By the grace of God Almighty, everything went as planned. The following morning, I ventured into town, as was customary, to confirm that the RUF didn't have the foggiest idea about our movement the night before. On the very next night, again, we started the move by trickle method, but the rain played spoilsport as we got caught in the downpour. It was a challenge to walk upright as the breeze intensified into whirlwinds. Even the forest was hit by an intense blow of lightning, creating a spectacular show, amplifying the shadows in the dense woods. Halfway through, the RUF soldier returning from his sentry duty spotted us and immediately opened fire. Any casualty to the RUF soldier would have definitely been the genesis of a full-fledged war, and we didn't want that. Hence, we took cover behind tree trunks. The RUF rebel kept firing till his last ammunition round, with lit up shots hissing under the dense dark canopy of the trees. He then rushed to call for reinforcements, which was a window for us to reach our destination.

Just as we proceeded, we caught a glimpse of the grace of heaven: the gales had blown apart the tree cover and created an avenue for our advancement. With thunder pounding from the sky, as though fired from a cannon, the rain was getting vehement, thumping the ground like gunshots, with massive drops hitting our bodies. Then, in the dead of night, by the time our last platoon made headway, the rebel reinforcements started rushing towards us, and there was a hot pursuit by the RUF.

Fortunately, by the time the RUF got its orientation right, our boys had entered the high ground. By first light, many RUF soldiers, along with Major Kupoi, came to the high ground. They shouted on our sentries and called for me. However, I thought it was best to let the heat die down.

After reaching the high ground, I shared the positive development with our Commanding Officer, who once again was annoyed with me for not keeping him in the loop. I replied, 'Sir, bouquets are yours and bricks are mine.' In fact, it was a very successful tactical move carried out by my company, executed without a bullet being fired by us. This tactical move opened the gates for the execution of Operation Khukri, and I always refer to this movement of my company as the 'Mini Khukri'.

Operation Mini Khukri was successfully executed due to the complacency that had set in among the RUF cadres over the last month. They had reconciled themselves to the idea that the Indian peacekeepers would neither lay down weapons in the near future nor would they go anywhere. The second reason for this successful operation had to do with the fact that the RUF was thin on the ground, as some of the soldiers had been directed towards Liberia.

As a fallout of Mini Khukri, the RUF had suddenly increased the presence of soldiers around the high ground, with more troops moving in every day. Yet we became more robust in the high ground, with two Indian companies, and reorganized ourselves to hold that area, to the extent of 200 by 200 metres, more strongly.

We constructed more bunkers to accommodate a higher number of soldiers. Trees were felled to make room for the bunkers. The logs of wood were used as roofs for the bunkers, which were further reinforced by a two-foot-thick layer of mud on the top. This was done primarily to provide overhead protection, since the RUF had the mortar capability to fire high-trajectory weapons. The high ground was covered by six platoons, and each platoon with thirty soldiers was holding a frontage of 100 metres; therefore, the strength of the troops relative to the area, by any standards, was very high.

We also rehearsed contingency plans of readjustments by moving a section (ten soldiers) each from every platoon (thirty soldiers) to reinforce the other platoon. To absorb this reinforcement, every platoon had prepared extra bunkers. We had eighteen rocket launchers, which were deployed alternately with each platoon. Depending on whichever direction the RUF attacked from, the rocket launchers could be moved to take up the positions so created.

Though our infantry combat vehicles (BMPs) could not reach, we had two BRDMs,* wheel-based combat vehicles, that were mounted with heavy firepower. We created tracks for every platoon so that the BRDMs could be moved depending on the direction of the RUF attack. Therefore overall, we were now solid on the ground to repulse any kind of misadventure by the RUF. Furthermore, administratively, we were slightly better than we had been at the hospital location. But scaling by way of one meal a day was still obligatory. Seeing our defences come up, with fortified bunkers and logs of wood as obstacles

---

* BRDM stands for 'Boyevaya Razvedyvatelnaya Dozornaya Mashina'. It is a combat reconnaissance patrol vehicle.

ahead of the bunkers, the RUF began to speculate about our intentions.

In the RUF way of fighting, holding the ground was never an option since they only practised guerrilla warfare, which is essentially based on hit-and-run tactics. A smaller unit attacks the larger force by stealth and after the attack, disappears in the jungle. Therefore, what was happening right under their nose was something new for them.

I was advised by Major Nair and all my officers not to venture out, since we had consolidated in the high ground, which was the most strategically advantageous feature in the entire area. It was also not safe to step out since my execution of Mini Khukri in the RUF heartland was not appreciated. I agreed with everyone's advice, stopped moving out any more and concentrated all my energy on improving our defensive posture. We could see the overall improvement in our bunkers, obstacles ahead and cutting fire lanes ahead of our bunkers to bring down effective fire on the advancing enemy. But as they say, the preparation of defence is never complete—we continued with our efforts to improve our fortifications and obstacles ahead of our defences.

We were getting well fortified, and the mood in both the companies was upbeat. But what was depressing was the uncertainty ahead of us, with no clarity on the future course of action.

The military observers were accommodated at the centre of the high ground in small bivouacs. They continued to create nuisance for us. However, ever since the guard had been deployed, the message was clear to them. Despite the indiscipline of the military observers, it was the need of the hour to keep them with us. Their presence was an asset for us, since some of them were from developed countries like England and Russia. I knew that the mere fact of their being here would at least draw the world's attention towards us.

We also created two volleyball grounds within our periphery, and the unit routine, including evening games, was followed within the high ground area of 200 by 200 metres. Major Nair and I were in a much better state of mind than before, despite the ambiguity regarding our future. The morale of the soldiers was kept under check with regular routine being followed. Though we made sure our men were well motivated, deep down we were sceptical about what the future would hold for us.

Sepoy Jayjeet survived as a result of immediate surgery, which was performed upon his reaching Daru. The only impediment he faced was that he had to walk down the last 500 metres.

#9

Meeting with General Issa Sesay

Almost a week had passed since the execution of Mini Khukri when one fine morning, the forward post of my company informed me that a lady, along with two RUF soldiers, had come to meet me.

I immediately reached the post and saw Sister standing fifty metres ahead of our bunker. I walked up to her, along with two armed sentries, to know the purpose of her visit. She gave me a message from Colonel Martin, that the Field Commander was in town, and since I had requested a meeting with the Field Commander, I could meet him today. I was in a dilemma. The timing of this meeting was immediately after Mini Khukri, and that created a suspicion in my mind. However, I did not want to say no straightaway. So I told Sister that I would have to discuss the issue with my headquarters. I asked Sister about her well-being and checked for the situation prevailing in town. She said everything was normal.

I called up my Commanding Officer on the radio set and informed him about the development. His immediate reaction was a big 'No'. However, he mentioned that he would further discuss the issue with the Force Commander. In the meantime, all my officers got to know about Sister's message, and they requested me to not move out since it clearly was an RUF trap. I assured them that I was not going for the meeting under any circumstance. But as they say, God has strange ways of doing things.

It was difficult for me to understand why our Commanding Officer, who was initially against my moving out, called back after having discussed the matter with the Force Commander and said that I should go for the meeting with the RUF Field Commander. He also shared the information that, as per intelligence available in the Force Headquarters, General Issa Sesay, the Field Commander, was in Kailahun town on that particular day. Our Force Commander, General Jetley, had been trying for a meeting with the Field Commander of the RUF since the commencement of the crisis, but the RUF Field Commander was not conceding to the request.

The Force Headquarters suggested that if he was ready to meet me, I must go for the meeting. Colonel Satish also instructed me to raise the issue for the release of Lieutenant Colonel Amit Sharma and the patrol party held by the RUF at Kuiva. I was silent as my intuition warned me against moving out of the safety of the high ground. I immediately discussed the entire issue with Major Nair, who very candidly told me that had he been in my place, he wouldn't have dared to venture out in this situation.

Before I could make up my mind, I got a call again from our Commanding Officer. He instructed me not to move out all by myself and take another officer along. I was bewildered; my mind went absolutely blank. I could manage to get myself together only once I reached our company's makeshift temple. I sought Maa Durga's blessings and prayed that I be shown the right path. Sepoy Vinod was in the temple as always, and he assured me that whatever I had done so far was as per the directions of Maa Durga. With her blessings, I could not go wrong in my judgement. I felt the inner strength and courage to go ahead with the meeting in the larger interest of peace in Kailahun, which I had promised to Papa Giema and every local resident of Kailahun town. My officers were taken aback by the shift in my thought process and again tried to persuade me against going for the meeting.

After learning about my decision, Subedar Fateh quickly walked up to me and held my hand for the first time to say, '*Saab, main jaanta hoon ki main hadd paar kar raha hoon, par main aapko jaane nahi doonga* (Sir, I know I'm crossing the line, but I will not let you leave the company).'

In that complex scenario, I raised a question to Fateh Saab, 'What about those twenty-one boys of 5/8 Gorkha Rifles who are held by the RUF, along with Lieutenant Colonel Amit Sharma? What crime have they committed? How can we sit back when our brethren are tortured by the rebels?' With absolute clarity, I told my officers that I was going ahead with the meeting and asked them if anyone would be volunteering to accompany me since our Commanding Officer had insisted that I take one more officer along.

Captain Prashant and Captain Sunil immediately raised their hands. I had to say no to Captain Prashant, him being the Ghatak Commander, and said yes to Captain Sunil, since he had spent a couple of days in the town and knew a fair number of RUF soldiers. I handed over the charge of our company to Captain Sudesh and advised him to take guidance from Major Nair.

I must have walked in and out of our company-defended locality many times. However, this time around, it was different. There was a double-edged feeling. I was anxious about being held hostage again, but I also realized that I had an opportunity to find a solution to the ongoing stand-off since I was to meet the highest military commander of the RUF. I bid farewell to everybody in the camp, a farewell that felt like forever. I looked at all the faces around me and thought my chances of getting back were thin. A cloud of gloom hung over our company as my soldiers gathered around to wish me luck.

Captain Sunil and I moved ahead of our forward post and did not turn back, as that would have weakened our conviction. Instead, we walked straight to the first RUF checkpost, where I informed the soldier about our meeting with the Field Commander. We were stopped at the checkpost till they got the clearance to allow us to move ahead.

Two RUF soldiers accompanied us as we walked through the once-bustling town. I was trying to gather my thoughts regarding the issues I was going to take up with the Field Commander. I was hoping that Papa Giema would be present at the meeting. We reached the town square, but instead of turning towards the town hall, we kept moving straight, which was not a familiar practice. I then asked the RUF soldier, 'Where are we heading?' In reply, he pointed towards a house around 200 metres ahead.

Again, as we continued in silence, counting our steps, I noticed around forty to fifty people seated outside the house, and everyone remained in their position even when we reached. I wanted to wish the Field Commander, but since I had never met him, it was difficult to identify him. Looking at a smartly dressed person seated next to Colonel Martin, I wished 'Kai goa ma', and he, in turn, pointed towards a dapper young gentleman, who looked younger than me. The young man was wearing combat trousers, white T-shirt and sunglasses. I again wished 'Kai goa ma'. There was no response from him—the deafening silence appeared to have lasted far longer than it actually did.

'Yes, Major, you wanted to meet?' the man in the white T-shirt finally remarked.

Thank God! The silence was broken. I was put in a spot, with innumerable inquisitive eyes glaring at me. Once again, all I could hear was the birds chirping as I couldn't come up with anything to break the ice. My mind became a blank cartridge, and I stood there stiff as a rock. But with God's grace, I reoriented myself and exclaimed, 'Certainly, sir. It's an honour to meet you. And if possible, I would request for a one-to-one interaction with you.'

Yet again, silence, silence and silence. But in that quiet, I could discern their gestural conversations when finally, the Field Commander stood up and declared, 'Okay!'

I was puzzled. What did he mean? Did he ask me to leave or wait? What did 'Okay' actually mean to these Mende people?

Thankfully, Jonathan signalled me to move into the house along with the Field Commander and Colonel Martin. I followed suit, with Captain Sunil waiting outside.

The scene inside was different. Everyone looked relaxed, and that was when Jonathan explained to me that in public, the Field Commander had to follow a protocol, by which he meant a hard look in public was mandatory.

'Major, today is the first time I have seen you this petrified,' Colonel Martin said and laughed. I replied with a formal smile on my face.

Now I was at ease, and with the Field Commander's permission, I told him all about the work we had accomplished in Kailahun out of goodwill, from the humanitarian assistance to the Guinean border patrol. The Field Commander acknowledged our work and said that he had declined the offer of meeting even the UN Force Commander, General Jetley, and agreed to meet me only because of our humanitarian activities. I further spoke about my commitment to peace and gave my word to the Field Commander that till the time I was in command, there was going to be no fighting in Kailahun.

The Field Commander asked me why we were not going back the way all other peacekeepers had. I informed him that if we were allowed to leave with our weapons and with the dignity of a soldier, we would go today. He said that there can be no double standards in the RUF. Moreover, if he allowed special status to the Indian peacekeepers, then the credit for it would go to General Jetley, the Force Commander of the UN, who was an Indian Army officer. He added that whatever happened on the ground was because of the incidents at Makeni and Magburaka, which were credited to General Jetley.

Sensing no headway on this front, I requested him for the release of Lieutenant Colonel Amit Sharma and the twenty-one innocent Indian soldiers held hostage at Kuiva. He agreed to this and gave a commitment that they would be released soon. He then asked me, 'How long are you going to stay like this?'

I replied, 'We have faith in God, and he will definitely show us the way. Moreover, if need be, we would prefer breathing our last on alien soil than returning to our home soil as cowards.' I thanked the Field Commander for his time and assured him again of total peace and harmony in Kailahun, come what may. I saluted him before leaving.

While walking back, my steps were quick, and I was trying to look back from the corner of my eye to make sure nobody was following me. I thanked Maa Durga for her blessings, without which we could not have been heading back. The positive takeaway of my meeting with the Field Commander was that our covert movement from the hospital location to the high ground had somehow lost its relevance for the RUF, since the issue was neither raised by Colonel Martin nor by the Field Commander. I thanked my stars for that.

Both Captain Sunil and I were welcomed back at the high ground with a lot of fervour and smiles. I was delighted to be back and more ecstatic than ever, since Mini Khukri was an operation that would be written in golden letters in history, and luckily for us, it had become a non-issue for the RUF. Now, my resolve to find a peaceful solution to the stand-off became more intense, and to do so, we had to be very strong on the ground. So once again, I got involved in improving our overall defensive posture.

In the evening, Fateh Saab walked up to me and shared a piece of news that was doing the rounds in both the companies.[*] He said that some of the soldiers were propagating the idea that since we were on a peacekeeping assignment in a foreign land, it was fair to demand that we return to our country the way peacekeepers of all other nations had done. Basically, they were advocating for the laying down of weapons and getting out of that stand-off with the RUF. It wasn't their fault. Forty-five days had passed since we had spoken to our families or received a letter from home. Therefore, I perceived it to be a normal reaction. Also, it was not clear how long the logjam would last. To top it all, there was uncertainty about how much longer each

---

[*] Here I must explain that a company in the United Nations is a blend of troops from all arms and services.

one of us could survive. We couldn't say with conviction that we would be able to witness the next day's sunrise, such was the level of doubt looming in our minds.

But Fateh Saab told me that the majority of soldiers were highly motivated and convinced that under these circumstances, whatever the Company Commander was doing was in everyone's best interest. Only a handful of boys were spreading the idea that we should lay down our weapons. I underplayed the feedback received from Fateh Saab. However, it stayed in my mind as I wanted to arrest the negative thoughts before they started demotivating our soldiers.

It so happened that the very next day, Captain Sudesh informed me that the signal operator had disobeyed my order for moving to the most advanced post where his platoon was stationed. I immediately called for the operator, who replied, 'Saab, mujhe mere apne Company Commander se order chahiye, jo Daru mein hain (Sir, I need orders from my own Company Commander, who is presently in Daru).' As an instantaneous reaction to what he had said, I jumped from my seat, opened his belt (a procedure of punishment in the Indian Army) and ordered for him to be put under arrest for disobeying my instructions.

Actually, what had happened was that there was a communication issue from the forward-most post to the company headquarters at the high ground due to there not being a signal operator in the forward post. The signal operators were part of Signal Company, whose Company Commander was at Daru. However, at that moment, they were under my command. The real issue was that he did not want to move forward since, if hostilities broke out, the forward bunker would have been the first to be under the RUF attack.

I wanted to utilize this opportunity to send a strong message to everyone: in a battle zone, there is absolutely no scope whatsoever for disobeying orders. I was conscious of the fact that everything was possible under these circumstances, including the option of fighting our way back as a last resort, and Fateh Saab's feedback from a day prior was a significant cause of worry for me.

I immediately put the signal operator on field punishment as per military law's erstwhile provisions, wherein the individual could be shot by a firing squad in case he disobeyed lawful commands in a battle zone. The arms of the signal operator were tied to a beam (a long, sturdy piece of squared timber), and I could see him pleading for his life. However, I had decided on a plan in my mind and accordingly asked for a muster fall-in of the entire company. The firing squad was ready, and only my permission was required to open fire.

This was when I addressed my company to tell them that the individual had disobeyed my order, and as per military law, I was awarding the field punishment to him. According to this punishment, the individual could be shot down by a firing squad. I asked for my company's opinion on this. The entire company unanimously requested me to give the individual one more chance. I asked for a commitment from my company that hereafter, my word would be the final command, and not a soul would question my decision. There was a unanimous 'Yes', and I could finally see Fateh Saab looking at me with a lot of admiration in his eyes. Ultimately, the entire company was back on track, and they moved with full vigour on finding a dignified route to India. I was glad, my plan had paid off.

The ordinary course of business was on at the high ground location, with no update regarding events beyond the camp's periphery—a sign that the stalemate was still on. It had been a long time since I last met Papa Giema as I had not ventured into town after my meeting with the Field Commander around a week back. But on that day, I somehow decided to move out to get a grip on the latest developments and pay a courtesy visit to Papa Giema. This decision of mine sure caused some anxiety among my officers, but it was vital for each of us that I did that. I asked my men what was the worst thing the RUF could do to me. I said I might be taken hostage, which in any case I was, on 2 May 2000.

I informed them that higher diplomacy had yielded no result. We had survived this crisis for the last two months, and if we stood a chance of a peaceful resolution, it could only materialize with my moving out. For once, they were all convinced. And here I was, heading for Papa Giema's residence.

It was a usual day, the soldiers stationed at the RUF barrier saluted me, and I replied, 'Kai goa ma.' It seemed like a long walk to Papa Giema's casa, as unlike other days, I didn't encounter people to converse with en route. Papa Giema's residence, generally buzzing with locals, seemed as deserted as the ancient ruins. He was seated in his carved wooden chair in the front yard when I entered, and as I walked up to him, his affectionate smile narrowed his otherwise big eyes. He offered me the famous African rooibos tea under the shade of the kapok tree and complimented me for the successful meeting with the Field Commander.

Over tea, I spoke to Papa Giema about our depleting rations, a significant cause for concern. Still, he sounded less than confident that there would be a peaceful settlement to the stand-off. We agreed that a solution had to be figured out in all haste as the RUF had taken a hard stand on the entire issue.

Papa Giema informed me that prior to my meeting with the Field Commander, he had called all the village heads to brief the Field Commander regarding the humanitarian assistance provided by the UN peacekeepers in Kailahun. Papa Giema's aim was primarily to resolve the issue peacefully. However, his attempts were vitiated by the tough stand taken by the RUF to ensure the disarmament of Indian peacekeepers in line with that of peacekeepers from other nations.

Papa Giema shared the news that Lieutenant Colonel Amit Sharma was seriously ill, as told to him by the head of the village where the Indian soldiers were kept as hostages. I was quite worried by this and requested him to explore the possibility of my meeting Lieutenant Colonel Amit Sharma. He told me that only Colonel Martin could facilitate this. I once again assured Papa Giema of my commitment to peace and said that I appreciated his efforts.

The moment I moved out of Papa Giema's residence, I barged into Sister, who met me with a lot of affection and warmth. Sister shared with me that the RUF had planned to arrest me the day I came to meet the Field Commander, and everyone in the RUF wondered what made the Field Commander change his mind after meeting me. She complimented me for being lucky and credited my freedom to the blessings of thousands of locals whom we had looked after since our arrival. She also requested me not to share this information with anyone. I inquired after her health and asked her if a request for a flag meeting could be passed on to Colonel Martin. She advised me that it would be more appropriate if I left this message with the radio room on my way to the high ground.

The RUF had a radio room with every company, and through this grid system, any message could be relayed to any part of the country. They communicated using sophisticated radio sets with enhanced range. If required, messages could be sent from company radio rooms directly to platoons. They always communicated in their local language to not give away their plans in case the lines were tapped. On my way to the company, I left a message for Colonel Martin at the radio room in Kailahun.

Meanwhile, our routine of night stand-to was further refined by practising various contingencies, by physically moving reinforcements from one platoon to another, and also from one company to another company, to better prepare the men to face any surprise attack in the near future. The physical activity at night kept all of us occupied, and the RUF posts opposite us would always make rather mysterious sounds throughout the night.

The fatigue and pressure of uncertainty had begun to show among our rank and file. To make the stand-to more meaningful, Major Nair and I conducted situation-reaction tests on the radio set, asking for the counteractions of various platoons to hypothetical situations of enemy attacks. My round at night to check the stand-to in every bunker happened at different timings. The boys greeted me with 'Jai Hind' (Long Live India) each time—the enthusiasm and energy levels were high. The grit and determination of an Indian soldier truly have no comparison. Despite not having slept night after night for almost two months, without an inkling of the number of nights we still had to spend here, the boys stood like a rock to beat back any RUF attack.

Here, I must also share the famous quote on page one of the Indian Army's 'Defence Pamphlet'. It says that 'defence is the most difficult operation of war', a statement that I always challenged while doing my Young Officers Course. Back then, my opinion was that attack, and not defence, was the most difficult operation of war. But now, one realized how correct the pamphlet was. The initiative lies with the attacker, while the defender only waits—a wait that can be frustrating. In our case, this was just the beginning, but I could already see signs of weariness as a result of stand-to orders every single night, with only the high morale of the Indian Army pushing us through it. Besides the white nights over the last two months, the primary cause for alarm was the uncertainty that prevailed, troubling every soldier.

At the break of dawn, the following day, I received a message through the RUF post stationed opposite us that Colonel Martin was in town and would like to meet me. Unhesitatingly, I got ready and moved out with an agenda to look up Lieutenant Colonel Amit Sharma, who was seriously ill. I was supposed to meet Colonel Martin in the same house where I'd met the Field Commander a couple of days back.

On seeing me, Colonel Martin gave a half-smile and said, 'Major, why don't you go back to your own country?'

'I love your country, Martin,' I said, smiling back at him. 'You're my friend, and I wouldn't want to leave my friend and go.'

'But Major, what about your food stocks? Don't you think it's time for you to surrender? What's more important than life?' Martin retorted with his forehead creased.

With lit-up eyes, I enunciated, 'Martin, we are the soldiers of the Indian Army, and we survive on our pride and honour, not food. About what's more important: always our dignity over a gutless life.'

Martin always marvelled at the spirit of the Indian soldiers and had immense respect for our soldiers. I requested him to be allowed to meet our patrol party headed by Lieutenant Colonel Amit Sharma, a request which surprised him to a great degree. He assured me that they were safe and would be released soon. Still, I insisted. Martin eventually relented since I was going within his own territory. He provided me with a guide. I decided to visit the same day and take our doctor, Major Murali, along.

I quickly returned to our camp, collected some ration in my vehicle and ventured out with our guide. It took us around an hour through the dense wilderness to reach the village where our patrol party was held hostage. I was visiting this village for the first time, and it wasn't Kuiva, as was told to us earlier. It was a village without villagers, nestled in the depths of a tangled forest, with several rickety huts surrounded by the malevolent eyes of RUF rebels. I stood outside a heavily guarded hut in which our Second-in-Command was kept. The RUF guide explained the directions of Colonel Martin to the soldiers on guard, after which I was allowed to move in.

The ramshackle door creaked open to a horrific sight. The crumbling brown wooden walls, covered with kaleidoscopic stains, were illuminated by slivers of light caressing the timber. Generations of spiders had laced intricate cobwebs around the cracked windows. There, on a battered wooden plank, we saw Lieutenant Colonel Amit Sharma, whose eyes welled up with tears looking at me, but due to his medical condition he couldn't even sit upright. He was running a high fever and could barely speak.

What I could gather was that they were all right till they were in the custody of Major Tom Sandy of the RUF at Kuiva. However, for the last one week, at their present location, they had been treated mercilessly by RUF soldiers. Lieutenant Colonel Amit Sharma informed me that the RUF soldiers kept discussing my camaraderie with Colonel Martin, and so he requested me for his release. I told him that he would be free in a day or two. Then Major Murali thoroughly examined him, providing the necessary medicines as it was viral fever.

After bidding adieu to him, we moved out and requested my guide to take us to the other Indian soldiers held hostage. We were directed to the adjacent hut, where Lieutenant Pendse, the youngest officer of 5/8 Gorkha Rifles, was held, along with twenty-one Indian soldiers. The Gorkha boys appeared to be spirited while dealing with the adverse circumstances, but Pendse told us that RUF soldiers had roughed them up and had snatched all their weapons and belongings. I asked our doctor to medically examine all our soldiers and found them to be doing fine. I assured Pendse and the boys of their release and asked them to keep up their morale.

Further to ensure high spirits, I gathered the boys around me and screamed with pride on my face, 'Jai Hind!' Their eyes burning with valour, the boys hollered, 'Jai Hind! Jai Hind!' 'How's the josh, my boys?' I hollered. 'High, saab! High, saab!' The thunderous roar would've definitely scared the life out of the RUF rebels on guard.

On our way back, I thought of how the Second-in-Command had actually started from Daru to get us released from the RUF, and here I was looking him up and trying for his release. The moves of the Almighty are truly inscrutable!

I was supremely distressed upon getting back to our camp, primarily because of the way the RUF had treated our Second-in-Command and his party. They were roughed up, and their weapons and belongings had been snatched by the RUF. They were kept like prisoners of war—of a war that had not yet started.

Ever since that visit, all sorts of thoughts swirled up in my mind, coupled with Papa Giema's not-so-optimistic perspective concerning a white-flag settlement to the ongoing impasse. To top it off, the rainy season was fast approaching—another deterrent to the resolution. Every year, between July and September, Sierra Leone is inundated with heavy rains. It is a time when the roads are swept away, the ancient green lanes are reduced to muddy quagmires and the country comes to a halt.

To make matters worse for us, the stock of ration was diminishing by the day. At best, we could sustain for another 10–15 days. With these thoughts in my mind, I walked straight to our signal exchange at the high ground and asked him to put me through to our Force Commander, General Jetley, without any clarity about the next word that I might utter.

Suddenly I heard General Jetley on the radio. The ebullient tone of his voice conveyed to me that till a second before he had not been aware of the feasibility of communication with us stationed in Kailahun. While being on call, he admonished his staff back at the headquarters, for not informing him about radio connectivity with Kailahun. He then inquired about our well-being and spoke of his efforts with the UN Headquarters and the Indian government pressing for our dignified release.

I was exasperated. Being in Kailahun, I couldn't prevent the capture of Lieutenant Colonel Amit Sharma and his patrol party. I told General Jetley that nearly two months had passed since the crisis commenced on 2 May. If diplomacy was any use, it would have worked by now.

Furthermore, I conveyed very firmly that now it was no longer a question of our release, since we could have been released on the first day if we wanted to—we chose not to. Now, the issue was the restoration of our pride, our *izzat* (honour). I requested him to consider a 'military option'. He was highly impressed by what I had said and asked me about our physical condition, to which I replied, 'Fighting fit, sir.'

He said that it was laudable how, being victims of such testing times, we still hadn't crumbled under adversity. Instead, we were ready to fight our way to dignity. I told him that we were never victims, that we were warriors who had decided not to bow down, soldiers who decided not to succumb under pressure, who chose death over pusillanimity, who picked the nation over their kith and kin, and who were, are and will always be ready to defend the honour of our nation.

He now clarified to me how he was fed a totally different picture of us in Kailahun, that we were not in a condition to undertake a military option to resolve the crisis as a result of our confinement for almost two months now.

All in all, he was delighted to get my radio call. He assured me that he would crystallize a military solution to the ongoing crisis. He informed me that hereafter, he would call me every day to get the first-hand ground report without any distortions. The radio call must have taken almost half an hour, and I took a deep breath at the end of it.

If I look back today at the sequence of events, this radio call deserves its rightful place in history as point zero for Operation Khukri. Our Force Headquarters came up with the term 'Khukri', which was synonymous with the Gorkhas, who constituted half the soldiers at Kailahun. Historically, 'Khukri' denoted a strong character; it symbolized bravery and valour and hence it aptly depicted every Indian soldier in Kailahun.

I was also absolutely amazed at how a crusader of peace like me transformed overnight and started talking about the military option. I walked out of the signal room and went straight to Major Nair to share details of the talk I had with the Force

Commander. Major Nair told me that Colonel Satish might not like my direct call to the Force Commander. I then pointed towards the boys, who were busy maintaining their bunkers, and said, 'These boys are our responsibility, and we should be willing to move heaven and earth for their pride and honour.' He was quite convinced, and we shook hands in the RUF style. He then greeted me with 'Kai goa ma', which, of late, had become our style of greeting each other. We decided to immediately commence serious preparations for a possible 'break-out' from the high ground.

As far as I can recollect, my radio call with the Force Commander happened towards the end of June, around two months post the commencement of the crisis on 2 May 2000. And as a result, Operation Khukri became a reality on 15 July.

I requested Major Nair to conduct a joint brainstorming session in the evening with officers of both the companies, to discuss the choices available for a successful break-out from the high ground. I then called for all the Officers and Junior Commissioned Officers of my company to tell them about this shift in my thought process, from a possible peaceful resolution to a military option to resolve the crisis. I smiled and complimented Captain Prashant, who was a staunch proponent of the military option. 'Captain Prashant, you win, I lose.'

I further asked him to press the accelerator on the Ghatak training as the probability of our success would increase with an incredibly fit platoon leading from the front. Fateh Saab requested that I not venture into town hereafter, a request that I rejected almost in a heartbeat as I didn't want the RUF to get even the vaguest clue about any sort of operation. So, I ordered no change in the routine activity in our company.

I explained to my men how in warfare, unmediated combat would invite confrontation, but a surprise attack would ensure conquest. In view of this, 'surprise' would be our most significant force multiplier in the actual operation, which at no stage should be compromised. With that, I further emphasized the importance of secrecy, regarding whatever we had discussed about the operation. Hereafter, what started was a carefully planned and systematic preparation for the forthcoming military operation.

The same evening, we began our first brainstorming session, to discuss the possible options to break out from the high ground location. I requested Captain Sudesh to moderate the discussion, and what commenced was the initial round, wherein every officer put across his views. We reached a general consensus for primarily three options that were available to us. The geographical location of Kailahun played a pivotal role in the chalking out of these options. The first option was to break out towards the Guinean border, which was just around 2 km away if we moved on foot and crossed over the periphery of Sierra Leone, or approximately 6 km away in case we moved on the track leading towards the town of Koundou in Guinea.

The second alternative was to break out towards Liberia, which was around 15 km away if we moved on foot, crossing the international border, and about 20 km in case we drove on the track via Buedu. The third option was to move on the road to Daru via Pendembu, which was at a distance of around 70 km.

There emerged a unanimous vote to keep the three alternatives in the same order of preference as mentioned above. The principal advantage of the Guinean option, besides the proximity, was the stand taken by the Guinean government against the RUF. The common point between all three options was the necessity to break the RUF cordon in phase one, which required very heavy firing on Kailahun town since the only option for track movement from the high ground, for each of the three possibilities, was to pass through Kailahun town. This was something that made me anxious, though I did not share my sentiments with my officers.

I did put a term of reference to whichever plan we were to finalize that our fully loaded vehicles had to move with us. The implication of this was that we had to follow the track. Another issue common to all three options was that the Ghatak Platoon, under Captain Prashant, would lead the advance, followed by other platoons.

I had integrated one of the BRDMs—combat vehicles with very heavy firepower and armour protection—with the Ghatak Platoon to lead the advance, and the second BRDM with the rearguard I knew the exact location of the radio room in Kailahun town. I wanted a detachment of the Ghatak Platoon to blow it up just before our movement as a special operation, so that the RUF's communication grid could be neutralized.

During our deliberation, several pertinent issues emerged, and I asked Captain Sunil to minute all the points in writing, since we had ample time to further refine the plan. A critical point given by Major Nair was the paucity of mortars, or indirect fire, which was essential to provide fire support to an advancing column; and this fact was further compounded by the lack of artillery. I appreciated Major Nair's point, and under those circumstances, the only option we could fall back on was the rocket launcher. Therefore, we integrated three rocket launchers, with adequate ammunition, with the Ghatak Platoon, to be the vanguard of the Ghatak Platoon, which was to advance by 'fire-and-move', acting like a 'mobile fire base' ahead of the Ghataks.

Another major grey area was concerning the evacuation of our casualties, and we decided to have serious deliberations on this issue some other day. I wanted to further think about the responsibility of the rearguard since the Ghataks were dedicated to the front. After a successful break-out, I predicted that the RUF, which practises guerrilla tactics, would definitely strike from the rear. So it was equally pertinent to delineate dedicated responsibility for the rearguard action.

I was quite contented with the outcome of our first brainstorming session. Our most significant achievement was that we could set the dice rolling and see a new *josh* (zeal) and vigour in all ranks so far as the preparation for the military option was concerned. I once again instructed everyone to continue with the same routine as earlier and did my rounds of the town. On occasions when I stepped out of the high ground, I ensured that the company's charge and further course of action were well understood by Captain Sudesh.

A piece of terrific news greeted us the following day. Lieutenant Colonel Amit Sharma and party were released in Liberia, sans their weapons and belongings. The decision of Colonel Satish to dispatch a small patrol party under Lieutenant Colonel Amit Sharma on 3 May 2000, a day after Major Nair and I were taken hostage, was most unfortunate and irrational. Their arrest delayed the execution of Operation Khukri, as any offensive action from our side could have cost the lives of these twenty-one soldiers. To date, I have not been able to understand the logic behind this blunder.

Anyway, for me, just the fact that they had been released was enough as the sight of the peacekeepers in their undergarments, crammed like cattle in a rust-bucket vehicle, had hit me like a tonne of bricks. I had witnessed it all as a hostage. How could the RUF treat my countrymen in such a ruthless manner? And, on the other side, even in a hand-to-mouth scenario, I was trying to find a peaceful resolution so as not to inflict any harm on the RUF's countrymen . . . Thoughts like these stayed in the back of my mind from this day on.

The situation at the high ground continued to become more challenging and stressful with each passing day. Despite our initial brainstorming about the military option, there was no clarity on the way ahead. Nobody had slept for the past two months, and due to severely limited ration, we had been eating only once a day for the last so many days, that too only rice and dal. We were clueless about what was happening in India; nobody had spoken to their family or got any letter since 2 May. There was no light visible at the end of the tunnel.

The military observers kept us on our toes as they continued being a hindrance and kept fighting with our soldiers, who were doing guard duty on them. I was constantly in touch with General Jetley. However, there wasn't any clarity on the future course of action. The only good thing was that now he was getting first-hand information from the ground, and I looked forward to his radio call every day, in anticipation of some positive development. I went through my ritual of the daily tour of the town and decided to meet Papa Giema in search of some glad tidings from him.

While walking through our company, I met Sepoy Vinod, who informed me that the RUF soldiers in the cordon around us were passing demoralizing messages to our soldiers, instigating them to surrender and 'go home'. Sepoy Vinod, our panditji (priest), told the boys that whichever option our Company Commander chooses, from the three available, would be the right one. I had never thought in my wildest dreams that whatever we had discussed in the brainstorming session had moved like lightning to every soldier in the company.

I asked for Sepoy Vinod's views on the best possible option under the current circumstances. He promised to come back with an answer after the evening prayer at the company temple, as only then would he be able to share the path God would have chosen for us. I instructed him to definitely come back to me and said that I would await his feedback. I was mainly unaware of the strategic planning and the cerebration happening at the Force Headquarters, since operational issues could not be addressed on the radio set, it being unsafe for communication.

Whatever we discussed on the radio was in Hindi, and acutely confidential information was never discussed since the RUF had mastered the art of jamming and intercepting radio messages over the years. With no knowledge of the plans being formulated at the highest level, I was confident of one thing as a result of my daily communication with the Force Commander: that a military option was in the pipeline, and it was a matter of time. But only God knew how long it would be before we started.

With these thoughts, I crossed our forward bunker and stepped towards the RUF checkpost. I said to the RUF soldier on duty, 'Going to meet Papa Giema.' On reaching the town, I learnt that Colonel Martin was present at the same house where I had met the Field Commander.

I decided to see Colonel Martin, and when I reached the house, I saw he was busy meeting 5–6 individuals I was unfamiliar with. Colonel Martin raised his hand, indicating that I should wait, and I kept standing around fifty metres away. They talked in their language, so I could not understand anything. However, I could sense that Colonel Martin was quite agitated as his voice was more high-pitched than on regular days.

After he finished with them, he waved for me to come. I thanked him for the release of Lieutenant Colonel Amit Sharma and the party.

'Major, why don't you all also go back to your country?' Colonel Martin said, folding his arms. 'I am cautioning you in advance, there will be heavy rains in Kailahun for the next three months.'

'Whatever God will decide, we will accept,' I said, looking towards the sky.

Without grumbling, I told him about the rough handling of Lieutenant Colonel Amit Sharma and party by the RUF soldiers, which I had not expected from the RUF. He said that the Indian soldiers had tried to escape and were caught by the RUF soldiers, who, in turn, mistreated them. He further shared that our soldiers were fortunate since the RUF did not apply the punishment prevalent in their law, otherwise a 'long or half sleeve' was definitely the minimum punishment for such an act. He excused himself since he had to leave for some urgent work, and I returned to the high ground without meeting Papa Giema. I was left with just a sliver of hope after my interaction with Colonel Martin.

Major Punia's meeting with Field Commander General Issa Sesay happened on 7 June 2000. It was the only meeting by any United Nations official with the Field Commander in the entire crisis. This meeting is also mentioned in the UN report that was prepared post the crisis. Furthermore, as a result of this meeting, Major Punia managed to get Lieutenant Colonel Amit Sharma and twenty-one Indian soldiers released by the RUF through Liberia, as was committed to him by the Field Commander.

#10

Last Letter before the First Attack

The next day, during my routine call, Force Commander General Jetley advised me to use the most complicated words in Hindi during our communication since he was about to divulge sensitive information to me. Thereafter, what transpired between us was disturbing. For a moment, I thought of refusing. However, General Jetley left me to take the final call before making the 'Operational Plan' and asked me to ponder over it.

Primarily he was inquiring about the feasibility of the Kailahun team being in a position to break out and reach Pendembu, which was thirty-five kilometres away. This was mainly 'Option Three' of the plan we had discussed, which all of us had agreed was a suicidal approach. He asked me to confirm by dawn of the following day so that further plans could be crystallized.

I did not have the heart to share this immediately with my officers, since I knew that they would have outrightly refused. Yet, the more I thought about it, the more the soldier in me favoured this plan as it was the best option to restore our pride and honour, especially after what Lieutenant Colonel Amit Sharma and his men had to endure. The other two options were to run away to either Guinea or Liberia, but this particular option meant that we would have to fight our way back, right through the RUF heartland. The only issue was the number of casualties we might have due to the robust RUF deployment on this route. I shared this pertinent piece of information with Major Nair, who was shocked to hear about it and said, 'Are they mad?' without batting an eye.

I called for all the officers as I thought it prudent to discuss the plan with them before giving my final response to General Jetley. The moment I told them about the plan, there was a massive surge of what I sensed as disbelief and resentment in everyone—they advised me to put my foot down. Captain Sudesh anticipated at least 30 per cent casualties if we accepted this option. I requested my officers not to share anything about the conversation with our soldiers at that point and assured them that I would keep their views in mind before making the final decision on the issue. The next day, I walked up and down the radio room, awaiting General Jetley's call.

Upon connecting with him, I suggested the other two options, of breaking out to Guinea or Liberia. He told me that they could be standalone options and nothing much in terms of support could be provided by the Force Headquarters, due to the distance involved from Daru. He further said—addressing the soldier in me—that he wanted to teach the RUF a lesson. I asked him to give me an additional twenty-four hours to confirm. He reiterated that the final word had to be from the soldiers stationed at Kailahun.

It was a tough call to make, but somewhere deep down I was all for teaching a lesson to the RUF due to the humiliation the

Indian peacekeepers had to endure at their hands. From Major Nair and me being kept as hostages to stripping our brethren of their weapons to now cordoning our company without any means to procure food and basics for our soldiers, the RUF had crossed all limits in the last two months. The mortifying experiences drove me towards replying in the affirmative, with the only obstacle being the number of fatalities estimated in case we went ahead with that option. I could not make up my mind and decided to take the final call the following morning.

The next morning I found Sepoy Vinod standing outside my command post with a megawatt smile on his face. He always greeted me with 'Ram Ram, saab' rather than the customary 'Jai Hind'. I still remember that on that particular day, he saluted me with a loud 'Jai Hind, saab'. He immediately shared with me that Maa Durga had given her blessings for our successful operation to Daru. I would not have believed him under normal circumstances but did so now, due to the strong intuition I had had for the last two days. My conviction kept reiterating that we would not have a single casualty.

However, I still wanted to speak to my company before giving my final word to General Jetley. A quick Sainik Sammelan was organized, where I explained the existing situation to my company. I told them that the options available were just two: either run away like wimps or fight our way back like true military men. I further stated that our rations would only sustain for another week, and so it would be more appropriate to die fighting than to die of hunger. We needed to break out from the high ground by all means.

I told them that they need not be afraid, as every bullet carries the name of the person it would hit and nobody can change their place and time of death as it is decreed by God. Finally, I asked them if they were with me and in support of teaching a lesson to the RUF by defeating them in their own heartland and taking revenge for all the humiliation we had undergone for the past two months. It was a thumping 'Yes' from the company, and I swiftly marched towards our signal exchange.

By now, we had clarity concerning the tactical plan for Operation Khukri. As per the strategy, we were to break out from Kailahun at first light on the day of the operation and advance to Pendembu. At Pendembu, we were to establish link-up with the force that was to move simultaneously from Daru. The link-up was to be established at the earliest but not later than last light on D-Day. Thereafter, we were to go into a night harbour at Pendembu.

By first light of D+1 Day (16 July 2000), an airhead was to be established at Pendembu, through which we were to be extricated by air, with the ground force moving back to Daru in the manner identical to their move at the commencement of the operation. In advance of the first light on D-Day, two British Chinook helicopters were to insert and pick up Major Andrew Harrison of the British Royal Army. Our Force Commander was to ensure that while they picked up Major Andrew Harrison, all other military observers would also be pushed out from Kailahun in the same helicopter. It was a bit of good news for the military observers; however, I had kept it under wraps until the last possible moment in order to keep the details of the mission confidential.

The most significant challenge for us in this operation was to effect a successful break-out from Kailahun town, and the only way we could execute this was by bringing down heavy fire on the town. This would cause innumerable casualties to the locals, but there was no other way since our vehicles could only traverse on the track, and the only track available passed through the town. This was the part that had troubled me constantly since the time I learnt of the plan.

The second challenge I did not wish to suspend until the eleventh hour was to clear the ground for a helipad so that the Chinook helicopter could land. Though we had removed some trees for the preparation of two volleyball grounds, a few more trees had to be felled to achieve a clearing of the exact dimensions required for landing a Chinook. I passed executive orders for the clearance of green cover around the area. As anticipated, the moment we commenced the work, which involved felling a large number of trees; there was stringent objection from the RUF post ahead of us. I had to move out and bury the hatchet with the RUF's local commander, convincing him that the trees were being felled for a handball ground. Hearing which the RUF soldiers smiled and asked me, 'Major, you no go to your country?' My consistent reply to such questions was, 'Brother, I love your country, and I no go.' I felt obliged to utilize the trees that had been felled and hence asked my company to further reinforce the obstacles ahead of our bunkers.

We had kept the news regarding the safe extrication of the military observers confidential, and heaven only knows how the British officer got to know of it and requested a meeting with me. I went to the area where they lived. 'Major, are the trees being cut to prepare for a helipad for the British Chinook to land?' Major Andrew Harrison asked.

I counterquestioned him, 'Major Andrew, who told you this?' There was no reply from him.

I could only tell him that the plans were not concrete for now, and we were getting prepared for all contingencies. However, since the day we started felling the trees, there was a marked improvement in the behaviour of the military observers as they were far more optimistic about reaching their respective homelands with their bodies intact—a rare occurrence in a scenario when you are cloistered by the RUF on their turf.

Our camp routine continued as was customary but with the additional work of planning and preparation for the forthcoming task. There was no slide in the overall stress levels at our camp; in fact, the stress levels had spiked since the time I had given the go-ahead for the so-called suicidal approach. No one, except our company priest and me, was convinced that we were not going to have casualties. In fact, talk started doing the rounds in our company that our headquarters was ready to accept casualty figures up to 30 per cent. This was a challenge that I had to address as, if left untreated, it could have had a significant impact on the preparatory work and also on the morale of the company. I was resolved to counter this grapevine on priority and was waiting for the ideal opportunity to convey a strong message to everyone.

When your mind broods over an urgent matter that you need to address expeditiously, the universe transpires to present opportunities rather briskly. While I was busy coordinating the core issues specific to Operation Khukri along with my officers, one of them questioned the plan yet again, and that was when I flew off the handle. Today, when I look back, I feel I was a little too harsh; however, I did let myself out with all guns blazing on that officer. I still remember shouting at the top of my voice: 'It's brilliant! We are five days away from the operation, and I still have my officers questioning the plan rather than preparing for its execution.'

I warned all my officers, 'Hereafter, if I hear any one of you doubting the plan, I will not hesitate to push that officer out to surrender to the RUF rather than being a part of Operation Khukri . . . There is deliberation at the discussion stage, when we are evolving a plan. However, once a plan is formulated, we simply hit the ground running to ensure successful execution rather than questioning the plan itself.'

While planning a war, you need to address the various contingencies that may spring up while executing the plan rather than rejecting the plan as a whole and calling it a recipe for disaster. And when officers question the plan, it has a trickle-down effect on the boys, thereby adversely affecting their morale. The message hereafter was abundantly clear to each and every soldier.

Post the conference, I could impress upon everyone's heart the idea that we had to fight for our honour. The officer whom I had admonished at the conference came to see me in my command post to explain his viewpoint. He informed me that he was giving his opinion for the safety of our boys and not for his own life. I appreciated his spirit while emphasizing that the life of every soldier was dearer to me than my own. I had already given a commitment in an open forum to take back every soldier alive from Kailahun, and I stood by my commitment. I became a little sentimental and further stated, 'Officer, you are a bachelor, but I have my wife and two little kids waiting for me back home. I should be the one feeling the pressure, as one wrong step can wash away the otherwise carefree childhood of my kids and turn it bleak and traumatic. If my own officers are not convinced and are not on board, how the hell am I going to convince my soldiers to face the bullets tomorrow?'

Today when I recollect this incident, I feel that this was very important, otherwise we would have continued discussing the best possible plan until the cows came home and still without any definite clarity.

I agreed that the apprehensions in our company were not without reason. The actual plan executed during Operation Khukri was not the best from a safety point of view, but it was the best possible plan under the prevailing scenario and the most effective way to teach a lesson to the RUF, who had never been defeated by any military force in their heartland of Kailahun until the Indian Army brought them to their knees. This later turned out to be the principal cause and facilitator for the RUF returning to the discussion table to seriously explore an effective, long-lasting peace in the war-ravaged country of Sierra Leone. If today Sierra Leone is a peaceful country and is progressing in the right direction, I can say with conviction and honesty that the Indians played a significant role in this and paid a mammoth price to ensure peace.

I bring all this up to say that if we had gone for the other two options of running towards Guinea or Liberia, we might have won the battle but would have definitely lost the war. At times, God shows the way. And that was how we decided to fight our way back, travelling over seventy kilometres to Daru through dense thickets manned by RUF rebels, where we were ambushed twice and were constantly chased by the RUF.

In the end, Havildar Krishan Kumar attained martyrdom while fighting the rebels as part of the link-up force that moved from Daru. He fought like a gallant warrior till his last breath, with his head held high. At times, I wonder how destiny runs the show—Havildar Krishan Kumar was the only soldier of my company residing in Daru's safe haven, while all our lives were hanging by a thread in Kailahun. But ultimately, it was he who bid farewell to all of us. Till today, I can't lose sight of when he had walked up to me in New Delhi to say, '*Saab, mujhe nahi lagta main apne desh zinda laut ke aaunga* (Sir, I don't think I will come back to my country alive).'

As part of our action plan from Kailahun, we coordinated the destruction of the RUF radio room by a detachment of the Ghataks just before our break-out, to neutralize the complete communications network of the RUF. As a result of my frequent movement in Kailahun town, I had learnt about the RUF system of putting all the heavy weapons, personal weapons of soldiers not on duty and their complete ammunition in one of the houses in the town. I realized that if we found out the exact location of the house and somehow neutralized it, it could assist our successful break-out from Kailahun in a significant way.

Prompt and swift breaking out from Kailahun was essential for our operation's overall success. Therefore, I again ventured into the town without a clue as to how I would figure out the location of the house where the RUF weapons were kept. Yet at times, when you move on a task without any concrete plan in mind, God shows you the way. Upon reaching the town, I tried my luck with Sister since I had not met her for a long time. I went to her house to see if she was home.

Luckily, she was at home. I shook hands with her and wished her 'Kai goa ma'. I said, 'Sister, you didn't even come to look me up! Were you not concerned about me?' Sister exclaimed with a forced smile, 'Major, I was sent out of town for some urgent work. You know Major Kupoi, my local commander. He is such a compulsive worker.' She asked me to sit. I laughed, remembering the few competitive encounters with Kupoi.

'So, Sister, do you carry your weapons while away for official work?'

'Yes! Yes!' Sister replied almost instantly.

'Oh! Nice. Is it the same rocket launcher that was strapped on your back the other day in the town hall?' I smirked.

She gave a lopsided grin. 'No, I carry a pistol. Those heavy weapons are kept in the basket.'

Almost instantly, my mind latched on to the word 'basket'. I considered it to be the right moment to probe further about it. 'Sister, basket? What is that?'

She said, 'Major, all our heavy weapons are kept in a house we call basket.'

I needed the exact location of the basket in order to neutralize it. If I continued probing, she would become doubtful of my intent. But I was ready to take the plunge as I wouldn't get another opportunity. 'Sister, where is your basket?' I inquired with a poker face.

To my surprise, Sister immediately pointed towards a white concrete building, a conspicuous structure amid a garland of thatched huts around 200 metres from her house.

I swiftly changed the topic. 'How have you been, Sister?'

'I've been good, thank you, Major,' she replied. 'Major, I hope you are aware of the rains that are about to hit Kailahun.' Sister looked towards me. 'I suggest you make the final decision before the onset of monsoon.'

I got up from my seat. 'Thank you for your concern, Sister.' I said that she should come to India some day, and she was absolutely ready and positive that she would visit. She told me that she had never even heard of India, but after meeting me she was convinced that it must be a very wonderful country, where people like me lived. She also shared with me that she had no aim in life, but she wanted to leave Kailahun since the town always reminded her of her husband and children, whom she had lost in the civil war. I consoled her with an affectionate hug and asked her not to worry since her brother was there to take care of her. While saying this, I felt a little guilty since I knew that in a few days, this same brother was going to bring down very heavy firing of rockets and machine guns on this town. I felt like telling Sister that I didn't deserve her love and affection. With a heavy heart, I walked towards the high ground.

Getting to know the accurate location of the RUF weaponry and ammunition dump was a remarkable achievement for us. Hereafter, we only had to come up with a concrete plan for its destruction, as, in my opinion, it was imperative to destroy it at the right moment. I considered it to be prudent to discuss the plan for its destruction with Major Nair. I shared the positive feat with him, hearing which Major Nair literally jumped in excitement to inquire about it. He told me that it was an essential piece of information and that we ought to come up with an absolutely infallible plan for its destruction. So, we walked up to a vantage point from where I indicated the target to him, referring to the basket as the 'quarter guard', a term used in the Indian Army for the building where weapons are stored. In this case, it was more than the quarter guard since even their ammunition was stocked in the same building.

Major Nair had this brilliant idea that the RUF quarter guard must be targeted when their soldiers rushed towards it to draw their weapons. It was an excellent idea, as this would cause casualties among the RUF soldiers besides destroying their guns and ammunition. We started thinking of ways to trigger the RUF to rush towards their quarter guard to draw their weapons.

'Officers! Major Andrew Harrison's helicopter!' I announced in one breath. Major Nair concurred, as the arrival of the British

Chinooks in the RUF territory would serve as an effective trigger. The quarter guard was within the firing range of our rocket launcher as well as the machine guns from the forward edge of the high ground.

We decided to engage the RUF quarter guard from the high ground itself, rather than sending out a special team for its obliteration. Additionally, I did not want to give this task to the Ghataks since they were already overburdened with several tasks in hand. We agreed that this task should be given to a firebase deployed at the high ground's forward edge. The base should open fire on orders and destroy the quarter guard entirely as well as target the RUF soldiers who would rush to draw weapons from the quarter guard upon sighting the Chinook.

The plan for the destruction of the quarter guard was drawn up, and I wanted to assign the mission to the most capable hands possible. Therefore, I called for Subedar Kewal of my company, who happened to be an incredible basketball player and had played several tournaments with me. I had a high degree of confidence in the fact that any task assigned to Subedar Kewal was as good as the completion report. So the moment he arrived, I explained the entire assignment and its importance to him. He asked for two rocket launchers and two machine guns with adequate ammunition, including the rocket launcher's illumination rounds, to light the area at night for accurate engagement. The weapons were given to Subedar Kewal. Hereafter, I asked him to observe the target round the clock with a pair of binoculars, to monitor the activities occurring in the quarter guard. Subedar Kewal utilized the next few days to further refine the plan and shifted the firebase location slightly to ensure accurate engagement.

On the day of the operation, the moment the Chinooks arrived, the RUF soldiers rushed to the quarter guard as anticipated, and Subedar Kewal waited for the maximum RUF soldiers to congregate at the objective. At the golden moment, he opened such heavy and concentrated fire that the RUF suffered maximum casualties in their own quarter guard, with all their heavy weapons neutralized.

As per plan, the Gorkhas were to ride the deadly infantry combat vehicle, the BMP, from Daru. On the other hand, the experts of the BMP, the Mechanised Infantry soldiers, were to break out on foot from Kailahun. What I wish to highlight is the strange ways of destiny and the importance of flexibility, taught to us in our schools of instruction, as the most important guiding principle for all operations. The Gorkhas are classic infantry soldiers trained to execute operations on the ground, and my company was Mechanised Infantry, trained to fight on the BMP. But now the tables had turned.

The BMP is a very potent Russian equipment, with tremendous firepower in terms of missiles, high-calibre cannon and machine guns mounted on it. There's adequate armour protection to safeguard the soldiers seated inside. One section of ten soldiers is mounted on each BMP, and it can move with a maximum speed of 65 km/hr and can also swim through any water obstacle despite its weight, which happens to be 14 tonnes.

I engaged in friendly banter with Major Nair, who was from the Gorkha Battalion about how the Gorkhas are really going to enjoy the BMP ride even as the actual riders of the BMP were going to slog it by way of fighting on foot while breaking out from Kailahun. I really missed our BMPs—had they reached us in Kailahun, breaking the siege of the RUF would have been as easy as pie. Anyway, the break-out plan we were evolving, despite being strewn with obstacles, was the finest in light of the circumstances. We had to put the BRDM, another combat vehicle, and the Ghataks in the front, and provide fire support with the mobile firebase of rocket launchers. A successful fighting break-out from Kailahun was the most critical phase of our operation.

To ensure success, the Force Commander had provided aerial support to the force at Kailahun through attack helicopters, which were to take off from Daru. Again, God has peculiar ways of testing us in precarious situations, and sure enough, the British Chinooks could fly in as planned on the day of the operation, but just prior to the take-off of the attack helicopters, the weather turned inclement. As a result, I was told to hold my horses. I remember asking the Operations Officer on the radio set to put me through to the Force Commander. General Jetley advised me to hold till the weather cleared.

In contrast, I was for effecting immediate break-out, since the surprise element had already been compromised by the flying in of the Chinooks, and any delay would have given the RUF time to reinforce the cordon around us. General Jetley did clear my request for an immediate break-out but with due warning, that in case we had too many casualties in executing a fighting break-out without the support of the attack helicopters, I was accountable for my decision as the man on the ground. My reply was a crisp, 'Yes, sir! It is my duty, and I will bloody well bring every single boy stuck in Kailahun home.' And I shouted the war cry, 'Bharat Mata Ki Jai!'

The operation was to commence at first light on 15 July 2000. Though there were only two days left to hit the road, I still had a glimmer of hope for a peaceful solution and wished to speak with Colonel Martin one last time. I was in a buoyant mood as my request for a meeting had been promptly honoured by Colonel Martin every time. Besides this being my last attempt at an honourable solution, somewhere deep down, I also had this desire to wish godspeed to Colonel Martin before facing him in the battleground on 15 July 2000. My request for a flag meeting got a prompt response, conveyed to me by the RUF checkpost stationed right next to the high ground.

On my way to meet Colonel Martin, the RUF Post Commander asked me to expect Colonel Martin at Papa Giema's residence. I reached Papa Giema's home hoping that Colonel Martin would be there shortly. However, an hour had passed without any sign of Colonel Martin, though I had utilized this time to prepare Papa Giema and have him take a stand in front of Colonel Martin to help pave the way for an amicable settlement to the stand-off. Alongside this, I kept praying to God to show me the dignified way out of this ordeal without any superfluous bloodshed.

Though all the arrangements were in place for the break-out, I was still open to agreeing to a middle ground as a solution to the stand-off, so as to not cause any harm to the local people. I had mentally prepared myself to walk away from the high ground with only our weapons and leave behind all the tentage and other stores, in case Colonel Martin agreed upon finding a middle ground to the impasse. The preceding three months had taken a heavy toll on me, and I had moved heaven and earth to sustain peace. I was committed to all my assurances given to Papa Giema and all residents of Kailahun. Therefore, I prayed to the Almighty to throw light on the righteous path so that Colonel Martin could make a decision that would be in everyone's best interest.

Finally, Colonel Martin arrived in the evening, and the first thing he inquired after was my health and the well-being of our soldiers at the high ground. I asked about his health too and prayed for his long life. Then, I requested that Colonel Martin channelize our collective efforts to find an amicable solution to the ongoing stand-off between the RUF and the peacekeepers in Kailahun. Colonel Martin took a few lungfuls of breath and spoke of how he had taken the ultimate step by organizing a meeting for me with the senior-most decision-making authority of the RUF, the Field Commander. He further stated that he had to go out of his way to organize that meeting since I was his friend; otherwise, the Field Commander did not meet anyone. He informed me that he didn't have the authority to alter the decision taken by the Field Commander on this issue.

He abruptly switched the topic and informed me that he was coming from Liberia, and that when he got to know about my request for a meeting, he picked up a bottle of Scotch for me. I sincerely thanked him for his wonderful gesture and proposed that if he had the time, I would like to share a drink with him rather than carry the bottle along. He agreed, but with the rider that he would leave in an hour. Papa Giema quickly arranged for the glasses, and I think this was for the first time that even Papa Giema shared a drink with me. We discussed general issues. But I realized that I was getting a little emotional while talking about my wonderful association with Colonel Martin. I even said that I would cherish our bond of friendship forever.

Shortly after, Papa Giema raised the controversial issue with Colonel Martin, initially in their local language and later in English, urging him to let the Indian peacekeepers go with their weapons, for the sake of their excellent work and contribution. Colonel Martin did not respond to Papa Giema's statement.

Instead, he continued with his drink while telling me how the situation in Liberia was getting beyond the control of President Charles Taylor.

He also spoke about how he had never experienced a situation like the one in Kailahun, wherein he had allowed individuals surrounded by the RUF to go home, though sans their weapons, and they had still refused to leave. However, he did compliment me and said that he was impressed with the bravery and professionalism displayed by the Indian soldiers. I said that I had no option but to stand my ground under current circumstances. I explained the disgrace that befalls a Company Commander whose company lays down weapons in an impasse. In such a scenario, my boys would still have a way to save face, by saying that their Company Commander had ordered them to lay down weapons. But what would I say? My one decision could bring disgrace to my nation—a nation that had gloriously fought for its freedom.

He seemed to have understood my viewpoint. Hearing what I said, he got up and shook my hand. He once again complimented me and stated that since my meeting with the Field Commander, even he held me in high regard. After this, he asked for my permission to leave, and on the spur of the moment I said, 'Martin! I will miss you.' This was followed by an emotional hug.

This was my final meeting with Colonel Martin. To date, I am unaware if he is alive or dead, but I respect him with all sincerity for being the person that he was.

Operation Khukri was to commence at the crack of dawn on 15 July, and my meeting with Colonel Martin, on 13 July, was meant to confirm that the RUF had no leads about the events that were to unfold in the next couple of days. Who could even dream that the Commander of a breaking-out force would enjoy a drink with the Commander of the enemy camp barely thirty-two hours before the commencement of the operation—an operation that was as secretive as the Swiss Bank? The RUF didn't have an inkling about such a colossal operation, whose curtain-raiser would be held in the RUF's heartland. Such was the significance of the surprise element in our operation that we continued with our routine activities right until the end.

The loading of our vehicles commenced under the pitch-black sky of Kailahun, where even the moon—camouflaged under the overcast sky—couldn't testify to the covert actions taking place on 14 July, a few hours before our break-out. My moving out into the town on 14 July was equally important, in order to ensure that the RUF had no hunch about our intent.

I went to the town on 14 July, just like on other days, and met Papa Giema and the other local residents. During this final visit, it was as though my conscience was smothering my breathing passage. My heart kept pushing me to give away a slight hint of what was going to happen the next day to the innocent civilians, so that they could leave the town before our launchers would bring down heavy fire on the town. They didn't have any role to play in the stand-off but had pushed for our dignified release. And how would we pay them back?

But what about the 233 Indian Army soldiers who had lived a life of torment for over seventy-five days? One hint would have cost 233 lives, and so I suppressed my inner hankering. I still remember Papa Giema saying that I looked more serious than on other days. I wished I could at least share the plan with Papa Giema, so I could save the man who had stood like a rock to ensure our safety. It was a conflict between duty and conscience, and there are times that I regret being in the uniform, which binds you so hard to your duty that your conscience has to take a back seat.

It's all history now, but there are times that I question myself and feel that I should have taken my conscience call to indirectly caution Papa Giema. Anyway, on that day, I thanked Papa Giema for whatever he had done for me personally and for all my boys, promising to see him the next day. In his wildest dreams, the fellow would not have understood what I meant by the 'next day'. On my way back to the high ground, I could see the locals covering the roofs of their huts with polythene sheets, gearing up for the approaching rains. It broke my heart thinking that some of these souls might not live beyond tomorrow to see another sunrise, so rains were out of the question.

I had to compose myself and reach the high ground location, where I kept pondering over the plight of the innocent locals for quite some time before I could focus on the tasks that lay ahead. The loading commenced when it was dark, and I had given priority to the loading of the ammunition and warlike stores. Sepoy Vinod came to me to ask which vehicle should be honoured with Maa Durga since there was no separate mandir vehicle. I instructed him that we would have a proper aarti (prayer) in our mandir after the loading was completed, and thereafter we would close down the mandir. The vehicles were limited, and the stores far too many; therefore, some non-warlike stores, like tentage, Sintex water tanks and foldable beds, were to be left behind. My officers had detailed two boys to burn all non-essential stores the moment the break-out commenced, a development that I learnt of only on reaching Daru.

A delicate issue had also come up: the number of personal weapons was fewer than the number of soldiers. Therefore, some of us were to go without guns. I looked towards Captain Sunil and said, 'If I hold a rifle, what would my boys do?' Captain

Sunil asked me what I would carry, and I pointed towards my black umbrella, my companion in all my trips to the town, though not a preferred choice of weapon in war. I had decided to put up my umbrella and march towards the town the next day. The length of the unfurled umbrella, added to my height, would surely paint a target on me, but it would also clear all inhibitions in the minds of my men, which was my real intention. I was later told by Captain Sunil that seeing me walk with a huge black open umbrella in my hand during the operation, the boys of my company were pumped with josh (zeal), and that fear factor was nowhere to be seen.

The military observers had a faint idea about the operational plan. However, they were clueless about their movement. I called for them after last light on 14 July. They all turned up in very good time, unlike on regular days, when they would take awfully long whenever summoned. Before sharing the details of their move, I inquired if they were aware of what was happening around them. They said that they knew preparations for an operation were

The Umbrella of Resilience: Major Punia's legendary black umbrella is still preserved at the Battalion Officers' Mess of 14 Mechanised Infantry, as a souvenir of Operation Khukri.

on, but they did not know the details. I thought of addressing them before sharing the bit of news they were searching for.

I told them that they were witness to every event here, starting from when the Indian peacekeepers first walked into Kailahun. We had tried everything possible to maintain peace and harmony in Kailahun in the true spirit of a committed peacekeeper. With no other way out, we had to go ahead with the fighting break-out from Kailahun to head for our Battalion Headquarters in Daru. Given the series of events that had unfolded over the past three months, we had no option but to keep the military observers in the safety of the high ground.

I reminded them of the circumstances under which they had walked to the high ground and how we shared a couple of nights as hostages at Geima, the RUF headquarters. Before any of them could ask me to wait for a few more days in search of peace, I informed them that I did not have the rations to feed them the next day. While I was addressing them, I could see each of them had the big question in their eyes, as to where they fitted in the overall operation. I did not have the time to continue any longer, since over the next 4–6 hours we had to complete several tasks and were literally racing against time. So I came to the point straightaway. I asked each of them to be present with their bags at the helipad by 0430 hours the following day and said that a helicopter would reach at 0500 hours to fly them initially to Daru and subsequently to Freetown.

When I went up to our Indian military observer, he told me to still rethink the option of fighting our way to Daru. I could only say to him that I would have been happier if he had offered to move along with the Indian soldiers rather than taking the aerial route. As a final word, I told them that they should thank Major Andrew Harrison, since the Chinooks were primarily coming to pick him up, and all the other military observers were his guest on the flight. The Pakistani officer hugged me and said that he owed his life to me. He further stated that he would always respect the Indian Army for its professionalism.

Having completed the preparations and coordinated every detail, we had our mandir function that happened way past midnight on 14 July. After explaining the arrival of the Chinooks to the military observers, we still had a few hours left for the birds to fly in. I decided to address all our boys and warned them against making any sound or war cry to ensure that the RUF did not get any hunch of our activity. The first thing was to inquire if there were any loose ends left. Thereafter, with all my conviction, I reassured them that each of them would set foot in India. I thanked them for all the support rendered over the last almost three months. I was happy to see them in high morale. I did not consider it appropriate to take too long, and finally, I shook hands with each one of them and asked the boys to return to their bunkers for the rest of the night.

In my bunker, while I was sitting on a chair under the candle's flickering light, I decided to pen down a letter to my wife. I was certain that all my men would reach India, and if that meant sacrificing my own life, I was ready for it. In the Indian Army, we have a tradition of writing letters to our loved ones before entering the battlefield. These letters are then posted to our homes, in case we attain martyrdom. With my conviction to have 232 souls reach India, I was ready to sacrifice my own life for every soldier in Kailahun. The flame of the candle guided my pen on the blank sheet of paper.

14 July 2k

My dear Anu,

The last three months have not been the same without your presence around me. The UN peacekeeping has gone beyond peace for us in kailahun and now it is finally time to fight for our honor. I hope Arjun & Mini are doing good and you, my beloved have taken charge of events around you, like always. I have promised my boys here that I would ensure each one of them would return home safely and with dignity, I have to uphold my commitment. I do not know what the next sunrise holds for me, I am sure you will be happy with my decision to choose our Country over you. The rebels have asked us to lay down our weapons, something we worship, and hence after innumerable failed attempts, we have finally decided to launch 'Operation khukri.' In case I make the 'Supreme sacrifice', ask Arjun to take the legacy forward and Mini must someday once she grows up must tell the world about our chivalry and Valor at kailahun. Its a relatively short letter as the operational arrangements are underway, so forgive me! Do me a favour, count the 232 kailahun Soldiers when they land at Pabm Airbase, and if the No is accurate, know that I am at peace! Hug the Tricolor wrapped casket, our love will continue in another lifetime. Forgive Me for leaving you halfway in this Life! God Bless! Yours for Ever Raj

After that, I met with Major Nair to discuss coordination issues. Both of us got sentimental. I pulled his leg and said I was going to attend his son's marriage maybe twenty years down the line. Fortunately, I did attend his son's marriage in Thiruvananthapuram, in December 2019, and both of us relived our Kailahun days.

#11

The D-Day: Operation Khukri

15 July 2000

Just before first light, the British Chinook landed as per plan, despite it being pitch dark. Our soldiers were flashing their heavy-duty torchlights, with the intent of showing the way to the Chinooks. Today, as I look back, I realize how unnecessary it was to show torchlights to a helicopter with night-flying capability! The second Chinook kept hovering to provide cover to the one that had landed at the area we had cleared around our volleyball court. It was a matter of a few minutes, and both the birds flew back towards the safe haven of Daru, carrying the overjoyed military observers.

The moment the Chinooks were out of sight, Subedar Kewal, as planned, took aim at the RUF 'basket', waiting for the rebels to enter the building. By now the rebels were charged up due to the presence of a helicopter in their area. When a huge group had entered the basket to draw their weapons, a single fire by our rocket launcher sent the building flying in the air like confetti, and that was the first blow of Operation Khukri.

Thereafter, thunderous rounds of rocket launchers and machine guns erupted from the high ground, blanketing Kailahun town under a thick cloud of smoke and fire. After every round of rocket-launcher fire, I had prayers on my lips, hoping that we miss the residence of Papa Giema, whom I had promised to meet that day. I had my fingers crossed, wishing that Sister would have run into the bush the moment our first round was fired; thoughts of killing my own sister for the safety of my men crushed me. With waves of self-loathing erupting in my mind, I heard a massive explosion right under our nose: the Ghataks had blown the RUF radio room and checkpost.

While our launchers kept firing without a breather, a sprinkle of rain began, as though this was something to wipe our conscience clean with. I looked towards heaven to thank God and requested him to overpower the wildfire ravaging Kailahun town. I had to stand firm and convince the Force Commander on the radio set to allow the break-out to commence despite the weather, which was coming in the way of the take-off of our attack helicopters meant to provide aerial support to us. The Indian attack helicopters Mi-35s, popularly known as Akbar, were to provide fire support to the break-out force in Kailahun. But we were out of luck, as the helicopter did not have all-weather flying capability, unlike the British Chinooks.

The Force Commander did relent, but only after shifting the entire liability for casualties of the Kailahun force on my shoulders, since, as per him, without the support of the attack helicopters, we were likely to have far too many fatalities. I agreed to pay the piper while advocating that immediate break-out from Kailahun was the only option left since any delay, now that the surprise element had been lost, would give the RUF an opportunity to reinforce the cordon around us. I was also baffled by the fact that nobody held me responsible for the devastation I was inflicting on Kailahun and its residents.

By now, the RUF had started firing from Kailahun town towards the high ground. The initial stepping out from the high ground, in the face of bullets flying from the opposite side, required some courage on the part of everyone involved, including the Ghataks. I was well aware of this fact. The 'first step' in any operation needs deliberate energy, and what follows thereafter is mechanical. God knows what got into me at that moment. I simply shouted our battalion war cry, 'Bharat Mata Ki Jai' and, with an open umbrella in my hand, I marched towards Kailahun town in a manner that had become a routine for me over the last so many days. However, today there wasn't any RUF soldier on duty at their checkpost to salute me; there were bullets racing forward to deter me.

The polythene roofs over the houses in Kailahun town, set up to counter torrential rains, succumbed under the fire of our launchers. The gravel road that was once made vibrant by the contagious giggle of the children was now cloaked under layers of sand. This, indeed, was a different day. The weather itself had changed: the hopeful sunshine was supplanted by a dark cloud cover, lightning and rain. The black umbrella was spread over my head. Its colour aptly depicted that it was a black day for me as a person, but it eventually turned out to be a glorious one for me as a soldier.

The eight iron spokes of my umbrella signified eight main lines of thought in my mind on that day in Kailahun, which I live with to date. The first and certainly primary one was the regret that I didn't apologize to Papa Giema for keeping him in the dark as it was a question of my soldiers' lives. The second was of a brother who couldn't save his sister, a woman I gave hope to, a woman who had no other family in this vast universe. The third regret was that I killed the people who stood like a wall between us and the RUF. My fourth cause of sorrow was that our bullets were crumbling the houses that took years to be built with love and care. My fifth cause of anguish had to be the fact that we as 'peacekeepers' were engulfed in a full-fledged war on alien soil, ironic as it may sound, a soil that we had stepped on with the hope of bringing lasting peace, but circumstances demanded otherwise. The sixth reason for inner turmoil was the fact that the lives of all 233 of my men were in peril, and I had to make sure each of them stepped on Indian soil safe and sound. The seventh cause of distress was linked to my rushing towards town to locate familiar faces in the piles of bodies scattered all around. My eighth thought was a desire: to have an opportunity to speak to my wife, maybe for the last time. What if I succumbed without hearing her voice?

But what was binding these eight divergent spokes was the crooked handle that my hand had gripped, a grip that spoke volumes about the determination and courage of our Indian soldiers. I marched towards the town at a robust pace, with bullets flying from the front but with no effect on my stride, which was far brisker than usual, as I was in a rush to verify the extent of damage caused in the town.

Captain Prashant shouted for me to halt a couple of times and then, getting no response from me, followed suit. My relentless steps, taking me towards the town, with bullets hissing past my umbrella, stimulated the Ghataks into a cavalry-like charge that set the stage for immediate capture of the Kailahun town square, which was our first and most important task before advancing towards Daru. The only track on which our vehicles could move passed through the Kailahun town square, and so we had to take the route under charge to avoid any attacks on our convoy.

Standing at the town square, I distinctly remember the Ghatak Satnam forcing his bulletproof jacket on me, and I had to push him away with all my strength. The jacket eventually saved him from being blown to pieces. In actuality, the number of bulletproof jackets was quite low, and I had made it mandatory for the Ghataks to wear them.

I was thunderstruck to see the ruined state of Kailahun. Under the debris of collapsed houses, it was difficult to count the bodies. I tried recognizing familiar faces, like that of Papa Giema and Sister, praying that none of the mud-caked faces lying lifeless on the ruined roads resembled theirs. I was literally removing heaps of rubble to confirm if there were some life symptoms underneath. Piles of bodies, coated with gobs of dust and burnt polythene from the roofs, were strewn all over the stretch that led to the town square and ahead. At that moment, I looked towards the sky, accusing God Almighty of pushing me to the brink and making me witness all this. I was devastated and cursed myself for opting to undertake the military option for our freedom. I had never thought that this was the price I would have to pay for freedom. My daily routine of strolling into town and meeting the residents flashed before my eyes. I imagined Papa Giema walking through the town's narrow lanes, in his monk-like demeanour.

With profound regret and remorse, I stood at the town square while we kept drawing fire from the west, which happened to be our direction of advance. I knew the exact launch point of the fire: Major Kupoi's temporary residence, which was around

200 metres towards the periphery of the town. I indicated the building to Satnam and asked him to target it with his rocket launcher. He immediately loaded the launcher and was about to fire, but in the process of pressing the trigger he somehow sensed that I was standing right behind him. I was so engrossed in trying to make sure the target was adequately aimed at, that I didn't realize I was standing in the opposite line of fire of our own launcher. With the launcher placed on his shoulder, Satnam yelled at me to get to a side, as the rocket, once fired, completely burns the area up to fifteen metres behind the launcher. I felt this was heavenly intervention at the behest of Papa Giema. He had guided Satnam not to press the trigger, since, in almost 100 per cent cases, during the thick fog of war, the man firing the rocket is always more focused towards the front, on the target, rather than on the rear. I was saved from being blown to bits, and we finally managed to neutralize the fire from the narrow lane in the front. I then asked Captain Prashant to advance by fire-and-move, that is to precede their every step with a heavy round of fire.

While walking past Kupoi's burnt-down residence, I could see our partially damaged Gypsy, which I had bartered for the evacuation of Sepoy Jayjeet. I instantly asked Captain Sudesh on the radio to pick it up on the way. Kupoi's residence was on the periphery of Kailahun town, and now we were on the track to Pendembu. Even though I had stepped out of Kailahun, the sight of its dismal state kept haunting me, and I considered myself culpable for it.

I once again thought to myself: Was this the best option, or could I have been more critical in my judgement? Did I do justice to the residents of Kailahun, who had stood like a rock to ensure our safety? Could there have been a better end to the

Kailahun story? How will the locals trust anyone in the future? All these questions kept scarring my mind while I walked away from Kailahun with a significant achievement under our belt, since the capture of Kailahun town was the fulcrum on which the balance of the operation rested. Even the weather started clearing up; the gleaming light of the sun symbolizing our first climb to the base camp on the steep mountain that Operation Khukri essentially was.

We would have barely walked a kilometre from the town when I discerned orange smoke against the benevolent blue sky. The smoke was our signal for the link-up with the para commandos of 2 Para (Special Force), who were air-dropped by a helicopter. Though I had read about 'link-up' in the many courses I had attended at various schools of instruction, I had never realized its impact and energy until I hugged Major Harinder Sood of 2 Para. The hug was like a new lease of life.

I gave quick instructions to Major Harinder to lead the advance hereafter and grouped the leading BRDM combat vehicle under the special forces. Now, I faced the real challenge to instruct Captain Prashant, who until then had been leading the convoy with his Ghatak troops, to be the rearguard hereafter and ensure the safety of the tail of our advancing column. As anticipated, Captain Prashant expressed discontent in a manner that almost crossed the yellow line of disobedience. I had to be firm and harshly ordered Captain Prashant to follow my operational command and converse with me only after completing the task.

The gist of Captain Prashant's argument revolved around the idea that he had undergone all that torture and the toughest training possible for the last two months, but now, when the actual time to perform was here, he was being ordered to guard the rear. I knew that it would not go with Captain Prashant's personality. However, having interacted with the RUF for the last three months, I was privy to their tactics of hot pursuit in such situations. Therefore, I simply ordered him, with no room for argument, and asked him to speak to me after the operation.

Our link-up with the para commandos was a signal for the main link-up force under our Commanding Officer, Colonel Satish, to proceed from Daru. The two columns from Kailahun and Daru were to finally link up at Pendembu, which was halfway between both locations. The Daru column was lucky as, unlike us, they were mounted on infantry combat vehicles (BMPs) along with other mobility vehicles, while our limited number of vehicles were loaded with ammunition. Hence, we trod on foot through the opaque thicket. Our vehicles moved on the narrow track carved between the puzzle of gigantic trees looking like skyscrapers on both sides, while we moved on either side of our vehicles.

Destiny has its own plan. It became clear to me after the operation that it was a last-minute decision to have Havildar Krishan Kumar of my company, located at Daru, to drive a heavy-duty vehicle loaded with artillery ammunition, which was ultimately targeted by the RUF in an ambush. It seemed like a foreordained unfortunate incident. The RUF rebels fired their rocket towards Krishan Kumar's vehicle. The rocket crossed from the co-driver's side and crashed into Krishan Kumar. He kept fighting even after the rocket had hit his abdomen. With blood oozing out of his lower body, this valiant soldier continued unhindered. He sped away from the ambush and parked the vehicle around 100 metres ahead, where the RUF wasn't present. Had Krishan Kumar not displayed this exemplary courage, the heavy vehicle filled with ammunition would have blown up, and its impact would have pushed the entire Daru column on the wrong side of the grass; there would have been innumerable caskets to be taken home. But his valour saved them all. The gallant soldier, Havildar Krishan Kumar, was martyred with his boots on—a brave act indeed.

To date, it is a mystery how he could have predicted his doom well before reaching Sierra Leone. It is also a mystery how the soldiers from Kailahun, a total of 233, could break out fighting through the siege of the RUF without a single casualty. Only minor splinter injuries were sustained by some of us. This was due to the surprise element of the attack, as the RUF had no idea of our intention as late as the arrival of the British Chinooks. This was further made possible due to timely targeting of the RUF weaponry and the radio room in Kailahun, which limited the RUF counterstrike post the arrival of the Chinooks.

Having successfully achieved phase one—to break out from Kailahun—it was now imperative to continue the same momentum up to Pendembu, where I was to finally link up with the mounted column of Colonel Satish. The next immediate destination was Geihun, where a company of 18 Grenadiers was air-dropped by helicopters to converge with our column. Geihun was twelve kilometres from Kailahun and post the link-up with the para commandos, we commenced our advance towards Geihun, with the para commandos leading the kilometre-long convoy of soldiers.

We were moving through the bush, which seemed impenetrable to us but was a means of obscure manoeuvres for the RUF rebels. Owing to the thick foliage and rugged terrain, the best option for us was speculative fire into the dense wilderness. We drew heavy fire from the tangled forest on our advancing column at several places, which was neutralized by heavy fire from our end. Captain Prashant had taken charge of the rearguard and was in constant touch with me over the radio set. By then, the RUF had reorganized after the preliminary shock of our fighting break-out and started chasing our column from behind. I had instructed Captain Prashant to follow fire-and-move in the rear end to ensure that we broke contact with the pursuing RUF soldiers.

The grave concern was that we were not able to break free of the RUF rebels chasing us; their bullets kept whizzing around us with a loud buzz. The head of the column was moving like a pincer while clearing minor obstructions on our way with ease, and the fire blazing from the BRDM in the front was a force multiplier. Though the rear end of the column had a BRDM, it was not able to exploit its absolute mobility, as the Ghataks would stop and aim towards the advancing RUF rebels before moving ahead and then repeat the action. So, along with the soldiers, even the rear BRDM would come to a halt every few steps. I was moving along with the para commandos, and we were a little short of Geihun when I received the fortunate news of the take-off of our attack helicopters. It was around 0930 hours. From that point on, the attack helicopters, flying on top of the advancing columns, gave us enhanced support and ensured better mobility of our column.

At around 1030 hours on 15 July, we reached Geihun, where our Force Commander, General Jetley, was already present, along with the company of 18 Grenadiers, to welcome us. His presence was a motivation factor for the boys and a pleasant surprise for each one of us. Before this day, I had personally never seen an officer of his rank step into the war zone without a care for his own life. Besides boosting our motivation, he could also manage to give quick operational instructions to me from ground zero. Before take-off, the General informed me that he had arranged a heli-lift for some of my soldiers from Geihun itself. The advance to Pendembu had to resume after detaching at least a platoon strength to halt at Geihun, to be airlifted by the helicopters, which I was told were already airborne.

I had four officers in my company, where Lieutenant Nitin Chauhan was doing a fantastic job in the leading BRDM. Captain Prashant was indispensable as he held the fort in the rear. Captain Sudesh was handling the company while I had taken control of the complete advancing column. Therefore, the only option left for me was to instruct Captain Sunil and his platoon to stay put at Geihun. On the radio set, Captain Sunil's voice conveyed a thousand words, and I did sense his resentment, which could have been expressed in these words: 'Why me?'

The column resumed its advance, but what Captain Sunil and his platoon had to undergo in Geihun was nothing short of the 'Great Escape'. They had to literally jump into airborne helicopters, rotors revolving in full throttle, as the RUF bullets chased their shadows. Actually, the moment we moved out of Geihun, the chasing RUF rebels had started firing at them, and they retaliated to hold the rebels till the helicopters arrived. Captain Sunil and his party were still looking towards the sky for some sign of a flying bird, with prayers on their lips, prayers which luckily were answered at the eleventh hour. Captain Sunil and the soldiers jumped into the helicopter hovering a couple of feet above the ground. This was the sortie of helicopters heading towards Daru, a colossal respite for Captain Sunil's party as they would land straight at the Battalion Headquarters in Daru.

The mighty column moving towards Pendembu resumed its advance, with the vehicles moving on tracks and groups of camouflaged armed soldiers prowling on either side while being involved in continuous speculative fire into the bush. At Geihun, I had tasked Major Baya, the Company Commander of 18 Grenadiers, to take over the rearguard from Captain Prashant, since they were fresh entrants into the battle.

We had painted all our vehicles from white to red oxide to ensure they were properly camouflaged. I know red oxide is not the colour of military camouflage, but it was the only colour available to us. On the contrary, Baya and his boys had painted their helmets white, a colour that belonged neither to the Indian Army nor to the United Nations uniform code. They looked like snowballs floating in an emerald sea of trees—easy targets for the RUF soldiers. 18 Grenadiers was the Jangi Paltan (Battle Battalion). They had recently returned from Kargil, where they achieved many accolades but had to pay a hefty price in terms of casualties. So we could immediately understand the intent behind the white-painted helmets: they were signs of peace and truce.

Little did they realize the futility of this entire exercise, since white made them a conspicuous target. Besides, the RUF had no mercy for 'white' under prevailing circumstances. In a little while, Captain Prashant informed me that the white helmets were no longer in the rear, and hence, he was back in his act of handling the chasing RUF. All I could say was 'well done' to Captain Prashant. Over the radio, I asked Major Baya the reason behind the sprint of his company. Major Baya's reply was the ultimate joke: he said that his soldiers were moving faster than others as they were physically more robust. The need of the hour in the rear was to stand firm and hold the chasing RUF, while Baya and his men were doing some route march.

Captain Prashant and his boys steadily held the RUF on the back foot while resorting to their fire-and-move approach, a task they carried out to near perfection despite some of them, including Captain Prashant, sustaining minor splinter injuries. The speed of the para commandos in the front could easily beat any slow-moving vehicle. They indulged in continuous speculative fire to the front and also to the sides.

Captain Sudesh informed me that one of our vehicles had developed a technical snag. As a result, my company moving behind the para commandos had come to an abrupt halt. I was clear that we had to touch Pendembu before last light at all costs, as staying in the bush for the night would give the RUF the upper hand and be catastrophic for us. Over the years, the RUF had mastered the art of guerrilla warfare and were familiar with every inch of the forest. I inquired from Captain Sudesh if there were any warlike stores in the vehicle, to which he replied in the negative. He said that only tentage and personal stores were part of the vehicle, and that was when I promptly asked him to push the vehicle to the side and fire two rounds of rocket launchers to set it ablaze.

In actual operations, every minute counts and contingencies develop every second, which must be addressed swiftly. Smaller losses are always more preferable than losing your soldiers' lives. While we were taking every possible step to maintain the momentum and tempo of the advance, the RUF was employing all measures to delay our advance and somehow force our column to spend the night in the bush. It was getting close to 1500 hours, and we were still 5–6 kilometres short of Pendembu.

Soon after, the leading BRDM suddenly came to a screeching halt. I was informed by Lieutenant Nitin Chauhan of my company that the track in front had been dug out and there was no way they could go over the broad ditch. Nitin had barely completed his message when heavy fire from the dense and thick elevated ground gripped our convoy. I immediately knew it was an ambush of the RUF, wherein they dig up the road and destroy the enemy with heavy fire. I asked all the soldiers to take position, and we started retaliatory fire towards the direction of the elevated ground. The para commandos moving right behind the BRDM came into action and started closing in on the elevated ground by the fire-and-move tactic. This was the standard counter-ambush drill undertaken by commandos charging towards a hilltop.

Even the pilot of the attack helicopter above us was quite vigilant. He immediately went into nosedive-attack mode and targeted the elevated ground from the side where the RUF soldiers were constantly firing at our column. The RUF had always been psychologically scared of helicopter gunships, and after this attack they were forced to flee deep into the thicket. We were fortunate to not suffer any casualties in the ambush, which the RUF had planned very tactfully. However, the significant challenge ahead of us was the twelve-foot ditch dug up by the RUF on the track, and there was no way we could bypass it due to the dense forest cover on either side. While the foot soldiers could still cross over, our real issue was the vehicles. The situation was getting critical with each passing moment as Captain Prashant was reporting heavy RUF fire from behind and last light was not very far. I instinctively looked up and found the solution hovering in the sky!

I asked the engineer expert of my company, Subedar Lakhinder, to advance towards the ditch and quickly work out the engineering stores required to bridge the ditch. On the radio set, I was fortunate to get through to the Force

Commander with a 'save our souls' (SOS) call, who, in turn, assured me of an aerial drop of stores by the helicopter. I asked the soldiers to take their positions and reinforced Captain Prashant's party with a team of para commandos to handle the RUF soldiers' fire.

The helicopter with engineering stores reached our location in a jiffy. It was a spectacle to witness our soldiers in Olive Green, camouflaged against the wilderness, blazing at the RUF. Concurrently with the attack helicopter showering fire on the rebels, the Mi-17 hovering twenty metres above the ground began dropping wooden planks for the bridgework. I witnessed the aerial drop of engineering stores in actual operation for the first time, and my full compliments to our pilots, who completed the task with the utmost accuracy.

I wish to applaud Subedar Lakhinder and his boys as they constructed the makeshift bridge in a snap. The entire rescue operation from the death-dealing ambush took about an hour. The precision with which Captain Prashant and his boys had pinned down the RUF in the rear, with the support of two attack helicopters, Mi-35s (Akbar), was commendable. The mounted column from Daru had diverted the RUF reaction, and as a result, before they could halt our move, we were back on track, with only the last leg left for us to reach Pendembu. Make hay while the sun shines, and that was exactly what Captain Sudesh did. He repaired the vehicle that was stuck while the column had halted in the ambush. My absolute compliments to him. Despite the gravity of the situation, his determination and technical acumen came in handy.

I was informed on the radio set that the Daru column had reached Pendembu and was in the process of clearing the town before dispatching a link-up force ahead of Pendembu to join in with us. This piece of news had a positive effect on our zeal, and instantly our pace accelerated manifold. Captain Prashant informed me on the radio that one of his boys had got injured in the crossfire, and I immediately asked Major Murali, our doctor, to attend to him. By God's grace, the boy was doing fine, and I was delighted with our progress so far, with only a couple of kilometres between Pendembu and us.

All this while, in the thick of the operation, the thoughts of Kailahun were out of my head. The heroism displayed by Captain Prashant and his boys was a matter of pride, and I was content with my decision to put him in the rear. Besides fighting our way through the RUF heartland, we had walked a little over thirty kilometres, but nobody looked tired—the hopeful smile of freedom, after an ordeal of over three months, could be seen on our mud-glazed faces. There, over the distance, we saw our men in Olive Green, swaying the tricolour. The Blue Berets beamed with pride. Familiar faces with wide smiles welcomed us. Captain Dipu Sirohi, with a bandage strapped on his chin, was the first person I met on entering Pendembu, and his warm hug was reassuring for me: a hug that exuded the warmth of freedom.

Pendembu was like the ultimate objective for the Kailahun party, since all of us were to be airlifted the following day. We went into a night harbour at Pendembu, with incidents of RUF firing at a couple of spots. However, our significant advantage was our strength on the ground, aided with the firepower of infantry combat vehicles, with their intense rate of fire. The infantry combat vehicles were deployed in the periphery, with softer elements tucked behind them. I had met almost everyone in our company barring Captain Prashant, who had gone to the medical room for minor treatment. I longed to meet him, to personally congratulate him on the most remarkable job executed by him.

While meeting every soldier at Pendembu, their moist eyes were a compliment to my commitment of bringing every soul to safety. Today, even after twenty years, I have not forgotten that feeling of accomplishment I experienced while meeting every soldier of mine at Pendembu. I felt like a parent who has saved his child from the clutches of death. I thanked God for ensuring the safety of my soldiers and restoring our pride and honour. It was a historic moment, as the Indian Army became the first force in the world to have defeated the RUF and that too in their own heartland, Kailahun. In fact, this defeat paved the way for getting the RUF back on the negotiating table, and this time for a spell of long-lasting peace in Sierra Leone.

If today, the people of Sierra Leone are breathing the tranquil air of a progressing nation, it was made possible by the Indian Army soldiers, who played a huge role in carving out this peace. I, as a soldier, had to pay a very heavy price for this. Furthermore, destiny had a prominent role to play in all this. I had to undertake this mission against my wish. We had to be deployed at Kailahun, where initially the Kenyans were supposed to go. Above all, we had to conduct Operation Khukri, despite my attempts to find a peaceful resolution to the crisis in Kailahun. Most of all, my heart sinks thinking of the people of Kailahun. Memories of Papa Giema, Colonel Martin and my dear Sister torment me to date. Life has not been the same ever since.

Nobody can understand the dilemma of a soldier—a soldier who was ripped apart by the bipolar strings of duty and emotions; a soldier who had to choose between the commitment of peace in Kailahun and his pledge of taking 233 breathing souls back home; a soldier who had to choose between the diverging paths of humanity and honour. Finally, nobody can ever understand the emotional baggage that I have been carrying for the last two decades. I have not been able to lead a normal life since 15 July 2000, and from one year to the other, my eyes swim in tears while my battalion celebrates the victorious 'Khukri Day'. I sink my emotions under the beating drums and the loud cheers of my colleagues, with a superficial smile plastered on my face. The sight of Kailahun reduced to rubble, with human carcasses crushed under the debris of dream homes, comes alive every year; and I have been seeing this sight since 15 July 2000, a date to rejoice, to celebrate the triumph of the Indian Army for its soldiers, as well as a date that makes me despise myself and detest my actions.

I live with the dream that I will visit Kailahun one day, to personally meet the children of the generation that succumbed in Operation Khukri as collateral damage. I wish I were less of a soldier and more of a brother, a friend, a confidant, or just more of a human; I wish I had at least weighed the lives of so many innocent civilians against the RUF's demand to lay down our weapons. My inner self was torn between my duty and my conscience; between my allegiance to the tricolour and my fidelity to the local people of Kailahun. In the tug of war between the Company Commander of the Indian Army and the peace crusader for the local people, the soldier of the Indian Army emerged victorious.

Whenever a soldier joins the Indian Army, he takes the oath to keep the nation first, always and every time. An oath that commits the soldier to fighting for his men, even at the peril of his own life. That oath is the only force that makes us pull the trigger, which is sometimes jammed by the opposite force of remorse.

I was so engrossed in my own thoughts that suddenly, under the flame of the candle, as if by a spell, I noticed something unusual on my palms. My palms were bruised with murky stains of crimson blood. Though the blood symbolized the bravery of the Indian Army soldier celebrating the glory of Bharat (India), something was not right. To me, it was the red river of sorrow: blood that wasn't a symbol of celebration but of mourning.

Would the stains ever wash? This was a question that stayed with me for years. The thought of Papa Giema, Sister and also my friend Colonel Martin distressed me night after night. While in Pendembu, I lived the entire journey of Sierra Leone in my thoughts. Even after we reached Daru, our Battalion Headquarters, I felt I had left something behind. I even took a headcount of my soldiers just to pacify my thoughts, but to no avail. My promise to uphold peace in Kailahun had been left unfulfilled. I felt I had to forgo the human in me and become a soldier in war for my boys, who were invaluable. I had to take them to their folks, their families, who were waiting with expectant eyes back home in India.

The bond that I shared with my men during those tough days was as strong as a rock, and hence, three years later, when I was approved to the rank of Colonel in 2003, I chose to wait for two long years, something unheard of in the Indian Army. I did so to be able to command my own battalion, my own men as a due for our shared history of Kailahun—I didn't want to part ways. Deep down, I knew that the bond I shared with my extended family, my battalion, was irreplaceable. Even while commanding my own battalion, or later commanding a brigade along the Line of Actual Control (LAC) opposite the Chinese in Arunachal Pradesh, that stain remained in my memory, though it had become pale with time, but I knew it was there.

It was only much later, in 2017, while I was on duty at Sirsa, that the stain cleared substantially. My division at Hisar was tasked to vacate the Dera of Sant Gurmeet Ram Rahim post his arrest in Panchkula. As the General Officer Commanding of the Hisar division, I was controlling the entire operation, for the implementation of court directions to vacate the Dera. Having cordoned off the Dera, I vividly recollect, we were standing at a crossroads, with options of either physical assault to clear the Dera or to give peace a chance and let innocent civilians surrender. Luckily, the man heading the army in Sirsa had the experience of being stuck inside a cordon for seventy-five days and could think exactly the way every human being inside the cordon in Sirsa was thinking. I am contented that I did not allow the operation in Sirsa to follow the precedent set by Operation Blue Star for vacating the Golden Temple in 1984. In my opinion, the collateral damage that transpired during and post Blue Star, with India losing its Prime Minister, was something that was uncalled for.

Hence, I took it upon myself to vacate it without a single bullet being fired. And so it happened. I am forever grateful to Kailahun, as it was because of my experiences there that we could save hundreds of lives in Sirsa. That very moment, a load was off my chest and I felt lighter. I believe that the innocence of the people of Kailahun and the fact of their demise left a permanent impression on my heart. Finally, I could breathe out years of distress that had cloistered me from within.

The people of the Dera in a way owe their lives to the people of Kailahun, who became innocent victims in the fight between the obstinacy of the RUF and the dignity of the Indian Army soldiers. Kailahun is a story of valour, pride and regret—a regret so deep that it didn't let me sleep for seventeen long years. It's a story that will stay with me forever. It was only on the soil of Kailahun that I understood the real meaning of soldiering, and how at times life throws a curveball and you get stuck in tricky situations with no option except to fight the people you love, to uphold the honour of the country you are devoted to. I have been in the forces for close to forty years now, and yet the tenure in Kailahun, despite being tough, will always be the jewel in the crown for me, as it changed me as a person. It had a deep impact on my heart, and I will remember it till my last breath.

Writing what I have written has given me solace, and even if the red stains on my hands have not disappeared, they have cleared considerably. As I stand in the witness box representing the soldier who performed his duty, leaving the seat of judgement open to my readers, I assure you that I shall most humbly accept your verdict, regardless of what it is!

For his undaunted spirit and display of nerves of steel in the face of enemy fire, Havildar Krishan Kumar was awarded the distinguished Sena Medal (gallantry) posthumously by the President of India.

As part of Operation Khukri, Major Punia was awarded the prestigious Yudh Seva Medal (YSM) by the President of India in 2002.

Even the Government of Rajasthan awarded him a piece of land on the Indira Gandhi Canal, which his wife has developed into a 'Kailahun Farm'. In her opinion, every grain of that soil will tell the tales of bravery of our soldiers to future generations.

Acknowledgements

I would fail in my duty if I do not thank Major Nair, since it was he who was the nucleus of both companies in Kailahun. He was the reason we stayed as one team despite facing the most challenging environment. In normal circumstances, a clash of opinions is bound to occur between two Company Commanders. Yet, despite the most adverse situation, we fit together like a hand in glove.

I also would like to thank my officers Sudesh, Prashant, Sunil and Nitin, who not only stood by every erratic decision of mine but were genuinely my pillars of strength without whose support I could not have done what I did.

Finally, it was Subedar Fateh, my most significant source of inspiration, who could bind everyone together as one team. God bless his soul. The soldier in him could not accept the idea of retirement, and so he went to heavenly abode on the very first day after bidding goodbye to the uniform upon his return to India.

Defying logic, Havildar Krishan Kumar could predict his future on the day we started from India. He will always be remembered for his undaunted courage, bravery and the supreme sacrifice made by him while fighting the rebels in a foreign land. For his gallant sacrifice and indomitable courage, he was posthumously awarded the most prestigious Sena Medal by the President of India.

I would fail in my duty if I do not thank General Jetley, our Force Commander, for planning Operation Khukri, without which we could not have restored our honour and the dignity of a soldier of the Indian Army.

The Kailahun chapter would be incomplete without my sincere gratitude towards Colonel Martin and Papa Giema. Their belief in me was the driving force for the events that unfolded since we first set foot in Kailahun. It's tough to trust a man from an unknown land, but they accepted me with such warmth and affection that to date, I am utterly indebted. I would forever be grateful to them for being such wonderful human beings.

To my handsome son, Arjun. Thank you for being my strength and taking over the responsibilities in my absence. You always called me your hero, but to me, you are my champ who supported his mother and looked after his sister while I was away. You are my star.

No achievement in my life can ever be complete without a mention of my wife, my best half who was the sole reason I went on this mission: a mission that changed my life; a mission that taught me what it meant to be a soldier; a mission that gave me the honour of preserving the pride of the tricolour on alien soil. Words are not enough to explain what my wife means to me, and the way she has selflessly contributed to my life is unparalleled. Even after thirty years of togetherness, her spirit amazes me. My beautiful lady, Thank you!

Finally, I am utterly grateful to Gurveen, Rachna, Gunjan, Vineet and the entire family of Penguin Random House India for accepting *Operation Khukri* and making it their own. They are the sole reason that this book could reach millions of homes in India. They made the operation come to life and made every citizen proud of the Indian Army.

Major General Rajpal Punia, YSM